PANDEMIC PARABLES
AND THE
NEW PARADIGM

BRIGHT
FUTURE
AHEAD

NEW
PARADIGM
AHEAD

JOY MARIE IBSEN

PANDEMIC PARABLES

and

THE NEW PARADIGM

Unafraid III

by Joy Marie Ibsen

Independently Published by Joy Marie Ibsen

UNAFRAID

Unafraid where 'ere you go
Choosing God to guide you
Let your course run high or low;
He will strength provide you.

In the darkness undismayed
Like the stars made steady,
When sincerely you have prayed
Heart and soul are ready.

Give your life for what you love.
Until death be loyal;
God will bless you from above.
Living will be royal.

By Christian Richardt

Translated from the Danish by Marius Krog

INTRODUCTION

Here it is! A new book about the huge effects on our present and future worlds as a result of the worldwide COVID-19 Pandemic, 2020-2023, and the surprising possibilities that are now before us. This book was written because COVID-19 turned our world topsy-turvy! I was surprised and disappointed at the conclusion of the intense pandemic. I had expected us to be joyful and celebrate our being able to be together again, to go places, travel more, etc. We didn't even seem more content.

Accompanied by catastrophic natural disasters due to climate change, the pandemic and its aftereffects have been a time of personal and political unrest, as well as new worries about the future of the world. I am disappointed that the ending of this major harmful epidemic did not elicit a celebration from us.

More than 600,000 Americans died during the first year of the pandemic. As of April 13, 2024, at least 7, 201,0681 people worldwide had died from COVID-19.

People talk about the enormous changes that the Pandemic caused us in our societies, but we haven't consciously looked at what is happening to us now, why and where we are likely headed. We have statistics but we don't have many personal stories that tell us about the effects of pandemic experiences. What has happened to us as human beings during this unique time? What will happen next?

This is my third book on the Unafraid theme. Unafraid I was a book of stories about people who lived in rural Midwest churches from 1939 to 1969 and the seasonal relationship of what was happening in their lives to the biblical passages presented. Unafraid II added messages from sermons during the pandemic, 2020-2023. Unafraid III (this book) concentrates on sermons about parables told during the pandemic, followed by the emergence of a new paradigm in 2023-2025 and expectations of the future.

Each chapter in Pandemic Parables is about personal responses to the challenging forces experienced during the pandemic, as influenced by the messages from related biblical parables, short allegorical stories that teach truths. The stories are not meant as definitive interpretations of these meaningful tales, which sometimes have a slight comedic edge to them.

These parables are *not* conversion messages. Christianity did not exist when the parables were first told. Jesus told stories primarily to Jews who came from several ethnic communities. In the parable, "The Ten Lepers," Jesus is a major character in the story; the other parables are told by Jesus, except for one story written and told by Benjamin Franklin.

Like many non-Christians, my Jewish husband was unfamiliar with the biblical parables as are most Jews. Characters in the parables (i.e. the Prodigal Son, the Merciful Samaritan) have timeless and herein timely interpretations and messages.

The sermons in *Pandemic Parables* are based in part on sermon notes from my father's, (Harald Ibsen) unusual sermon notes stored in an old wooden file cabinet. The interpretations help primarily Zoom listeners overcome fears and find meaning as well as more enjoyment in their lives. The power in Harald Ibsen's sermons in his notes is inspired by the theologian and educator N.F.S. Grundtvig (1783-1813) who was central to my father's life and has also been an inspiration to me. I have been further influenced by the new Mary Magdalena movement in the 21st century, restoring The New Divine Feminine Energy to world cultures.

I chose parables as the framework for writing about the pandemic because adjusting to evolutionary new realities requires the spiritual transformation which parables teach.

The sermons are presented by a fictional clergywoman, Pastor Maria, who serves a non-denominational, unnamed church in Albuquerque, NM. Pastor Maria is an imagined gracious clergywoman of the same general generation as my father's seven granddaughters.

In short, this is a book about challenges and wisdom teachings from the 2021-2023 COVID-19 pandemic, which were followed by unexpected political and personal unrest and finally the presentation of a New Paradigm for the new era which is unlike any other era! Enjoy!

DEDICATION

With gratitude to my parents,
Harald and Asta Juhl Ibsen

My father, Harald Ibsen, taught me how to ride a bike. I learned how to steer and how to choose a direction - what to notice, when to pedal ahead, how to put on the brakes, and how to be cautious, and not be afraid.

My father taught me how to drive a two-wheeler, in 1948

Next to the highway, we had a long hill outside our home. One day, I went bravely down the hill's sidewalks on roller skates. On the way down, I fell and skinned my knees and came home crying loudly. My mother put band-aids on my legs and sent me right back. I did not want to go back. She insisted that I try again!

"Try Again" was a lesson I never forgot. I learned to bike and skate and also managed other important accomplishments. My mother and father gave just the right amount of support-- not too much, not too little.

TABLE OF CONTENTS

APPENDIX

CHAPTER 1

The Pharisee and the Publican

Dan, Consuela and Nikia Forester

Sunday morning Dan Forester stepped out of the patio doors of his stylish stucco and glass home. *I should have risen earlier and gone for a swim*, he thought, admiring his swimming pool with its handsome sparkling waterfall. The water would be refreshing, neither too warm nor too cold, and a morning swim was one luxury Dan truly enjoyed. He also liked having Sunday breakfast with his wife, Consuela, who would soon be coming out to join him. Meanwhile, Dan would make sure the giant computer screen was Zoom-ready.

The attractive covered area attached to their home provided a large outside theater where the couple, Consuela's daughter and their many friends, could comfortably watch movies, cheer and critique football and soccer games, and enjoy a casual meal and the bar as well. On Sunday morning, it was a place where they could go to church.

Dan switched on the computer monitor, selected Zoom, inserted the correct ID numbers and was soon welcomed into the church's waiting room. Consuela soon would be joining him after applying her make-up and brushing the cascades of dark brown hair that framed her elegant profile.

As for Nikia, his teenage stepdaughter, he didn't expect to see her until services were over.

On the far side of the pool, from the patio off the bedroom wing, Dan saw Consuela coming toward him. After three years of marriage, Dan still congratulated himself for being married to a gorgeous woman who provided not only companionship but remarkable business acumen.

Consuela was 15 years younger than Dan and had much less business experience, but he was grateful to have a smart, energetic partner-wife. Because of COVID-19, his restaurant business was now more challenging than he or anyone else had expected.

Dan suspected some of his friends criticized him for marrying the manager/hostess of his prime restaurant, but Dan considered it the best damn decision he ever made. The couple now owned three restaurants in the Albuquerque area, but only one was currently open, and serving only 25% capacity indoors, due to the COVID-19 virus. Fortunately, they had a popular outdoor patio as well.

The other two restaurants were restricted to delivery, take-out and curb services. They were surviving, but Dan couldn't help but worry. The time could soon come when they would need to lay off more people. If the damn virus was not soon under control, and restrictions remained, they could be facing bankruptcy in six months.

Dan was thankful that his former wife Emma, who had passed away five years ago, missed witnessing what could be happening to the dreams they built.

Instead of cancer, the worrying would have killed her. COVID-19 was like an economic cancer--hard to control and impossible to eradicate. The prescribed treatment (restricting his business) was almost as lethal to the economy as the disease.

"Beautiful morning," Consuela said, before planting a kiss on his cheek. "Ah, I'm just in time," she said looking at the screen. It indicated forty-some participants as she took a seat next to Dan. Consuela wore her favorite sundress; she did not worry about what she wore when on Zoom.

Dan reached over and squeezed her hand. Maybe they would go for a swim after the services. He would enjoy that! Although a swim accentuated their muscle-tone-age difference, he could still outswim Consuela. Winning racing laps made him feel 10 years younger.

The couple's video image now appeared in the upper left-hand corner of the computer screen; other Zoom watchers began to fill up the video gallery of photos as more people were tuned in to the services. Several people, including Dan and Consuela, offered "Good Morning" greetings to other participants until Pastor Maria suddenly appeared on the full screen.

Dan liked Pastor Maria; he had been on the search committee that recommended her to the congregation. She was still fairly new to the church and like Consuela, seemed able to meet the challenges brought by the unexpected COVID-19. The two women admired each other. Both were dependable and excelled in their work despite the many unknowns.

"Welcome, everyone!" Pastor Maria said smiling. "We are so glad you could join us for services this morning. What a beautiful day! While we are scattered around the area, some of you are joining us from out of state, we are together as a congregation. We will begin by singing Hymn Number 256, "God is Here.""

The organ boomed out an introduction as the screen displayed a video of a half dozen masked choir members.

There was something weird about not seeing their entire faces; they looked like bandits, but they sounded good!

*"God is Here!"*they sang: *"God is Here! As we your people meet to offer praise and prayer."*

Dan couldn't help but think of March 8th, more than two months ago, when pews still cradled members of the congregation in their chosen seats. Rather than the last day to sit together in church, it was ironically the first day of daylight-saving times, with an extra hour of light. At the time, no one knew it would be the last Sunday they would be together in the sanctuary for God knows how long. Everyone that morning took church services for granted, assuming all would be able to come back next week or perhaps the next. There had been no reason to say goodbye, to wish each other well, to endure the unanticipated and uncharted journeys they would be facing.

But it was not going to ever be the same. The entire globe and everyone in it would forever be changed.

The following Sunday, there were no church services. Choir practice was canceled along with thousands of other scheduled rehearsals. Businesses were closed including Dan's Southwest Eatery, his primary restaurant. Consuela's yoga class was over. Long-established people's habits were disallowed for an unknown length of time.

By the following Monday, public schools were closed, and the first stay-at-home order took effect. Three days later, on March 19th, all the gyms in New Mexico were also closed. By March 24th a downward nationwide economic slide was in full force.

Dan, who had a strong baritone voice, sang along with the choir, at first a bit self-consciously, but after he was accustomed to hearing his voice, he sang out more confidently. By the second verse, Consuela joined him. There had been a time when she had refused to sing because she was not familiar with the hymns and lacked confidence in her singing ability.

As for Dan, he liked attending church from his own home, with no one beside him except this beautiful woman who would now sing with him. If it weren't for the COVID-19 virus ruining their livelihood, he might wish "Zoom-church" would continue forever!

Pastor Maria introduced the sermon as part of a parable series. Dan agreed that parables were a good theme, especially for the summer, but was disappointed when he realized what the day's sermon parable was about.

It was one of those damn stories that favored the lower class instead of the guy who was successful and worked hard for what he achieved. Dan was sick and tired of all the sympathy offered for people who in his opinion didn't deserve it.

Pastor Maria began by reading the scripture from Luke 18:10-14.

> *"Two men went up to the temple to pray, one a Pharisee and the other a tax collector. The Pharisee, standing by himself, was praying thus, 'God, I thank you that I am not like other people: thieves, rogues, adulterers, or even like this tax collector. I fast twice a week; I give a tenth of all my income.' But the tax collector, standing far off, would not even look up to heaven, but was beating his breast and saying, 'God, be merciful to me, a sinner!' I tell you, this man went down to his home justified rather than the other; for all*

who exalt themselves will be humbled, but all
who humble themselves will be exalted."

Having read the scripture, Pastor Maria began her sermon:

"This story is one of the most daring parables
Jesus told. It is primarily addressed to self-satisfied
people who believe they are righteous and good, and
who look down on almost everyone else. Often they are
angry people who feel unappreciated. The story is full
of rebukes for people who are overconfident and proud
of themselves. It is a story full of courage and comfort
for people who have lost confidence in themselves and
who suffer under the burden of self-contempt.

"We have several great contrasts in this story."

Dan leaned over to Consuela and said," Two men walk
into a bar, I mean, a church. One is a success and the other a
loser. Guess which one God favors?"

"SHHHH," said Consuela to Dan, not looking at him.
"Listen to the pastor." She kept looking straight ahead.

"Everyone has some good qualities; let's not be
too critical. The Pharisee is religious; he is a member of
the synagogue. He believes people cannot live by bread
alone. He is aware of the forces in society that shape
our character and safeguard our civilization.

"But he is not a saint. The Pharisee appears to
be an upright member of society and probably is honest
in his business dealings. He says he is not an

extortioner, which is certainly a low bar. Just because he is not a thief, doesn't mean he does a lot of good. But he shares his wealth; he gives tithes.

"The Pharisee describes himself as a decent man, unlike the publican who is at the bottom of the social ladder.

"The publican is not someone to admire. A servant of Rome, he extracts taxes from people who hate him because of it. The publican doesn't claim that he is not an extortioner. He may well have cheated while collecting money for Rome, possibly inflating the amount he extracted in order to keep some for himself. Rome was the people's enemy; it is likely that some of the money he collected was for unjust purposes.

"The prayers of the two men are very self-revealing. The Pharisee prays, 'God I thank thee that I am not as other people are. I am not an extortioner. I am not unjust. I am not an adulterer. I fast twice a week. I give tithes.' He approves of himself, and he disapproves of his fellowmen. In other words, he thinks he is better than everyone else.

"The equality of humanity is something the Pharisee does not believe in. He does not understand that while there are differences between people, fundamentally we are all equal; we are the same.

"Each of us has qualities like Judas, and each of us has qualities like St. Paul's.

"We find the Pharisee's self-admiration offensive and his prayer ridiculous. He is not asking God for anything, but rather telling God what a good person he is.

"He begins his prayer, 'I thank thee, God,' but does not seem to have a sense of God's presence. Although he says he is thankful, he doesn't seem to feel very grateful. He does not ask for guidance. Rather, it is as if God should appreciate him for being such a fine, successful person.

"The Pharisee not only lacks compassion; he seems to rejoice over how bad the other fellow is. He has no sense of his own sin or shortcomings; he has no sense of God. "

Dan looked at Consuela and shrugged his shoulders with a gesture of "See what I mean."

"Sin includes much more than deeds such as extortion and adultery. Sin is separation from God; sin is caused by not loving God with our hearts and souls, and by not loving our neighbors as ourselves. That is what sin is.

"The publican 's prayer is different. He has not come to report on his good behavior as if God were Santa Claus. He is in trouble, and he needs help. He claims no superiority and does not look around for someone worse than he is to hide behind.

"At this moment the publican is aware of only two beings in the world, God and himself. His prayer is a confession of sin. He has not only done something wrong, he is wrongful. There are no excuses. 'God be merciful to me, a sinner,' is his simple prayer.

"We have no details, but we sense how heavy his burden is.

"Now let's consider the difference in God's responses to them and the differences in what they receive from being at the temple.

"First, the Pharisee. What a tragedy to stand before a loving God who is eager to help, to bless him and for that person to receive nothing!

"It is not because God does not love him. It is because the Pharisee is not able to accept what God longs to give. The Pharisee is so full of himself there is no room left in his heart for God.

"When the Pharisee comes to the temple to pray he is conceited, critical, and unbrotherly. When he leaves the temple, he is conceited, critical and unbrotherly."

Consuela moved her hand to grasp Dan's hand. She looked at him questioningly but now it was Dan who was staring straight ahead.

"The publican leaves the temple justified, pardoned, cleansed, reborn. The publican's prayer, 'Lord be merciful to me, a sinner,' is a prayer for all of us. When genuine and heartfelt, the prayer benefits the worst of us, and it benefits the best of us.

"When it comes to loving the lord with all our heart and soul and our neighbor as ourselves, we each and all have challenges.

"The publican is often described as a meek person. If we understand what meek means, it is an accurate description of him, especially when he leaves the temple.

"'Blessed are the meek' is the most misunderstood virtue in the Beatitudes. 'Blessed are the meek for they will inherit the earth' does not refer to people who lack confidence in their self-worth.

"Martin Luther translates this quality in the beatitude with a German word which means sweet-tempered. A more accurate translation than 'meek' would be 'Blessed are the debonair'-- carefree, lighthearted!

"A strong faith in God and a strong love for our neighbors and ourselves enables us to be carefree and lighthearted. Debonair people often have deep faith

"Christ did not come to save the righteous. If we say or think we have no sin, we deceive ourselves; we are like the Pharisee who is unable to ask, receive God's help and guidance.

"Let us each pray, God be merciful to me, a sinner.

"Help us to be debonair.

"Amen."

Just as Pastor Maria was completing her sermon, fourteen-year-old Nikia came outside, her dark brown hair pulled back in a snug ponytail, her facial expression pouting.

Above her elbow on her right arm, an engraved unicorn tattoo welcomed onlookers.

Smiling, always smiling, Nikia, wearing her bikini, was about to jump in the water, but she looked up and instead of diving into the water decided to say good morning to her mother and Dan.

Nikia sat down beside her mother just in time to hear the last part of the sermon.

She waited until Pastor Maria finished the prayer, thanking God for the day, asking for guidance "in these difficult times," and praying for individual members of the congregation who had requested prayers.

As a video of the church's praise band began playing an offertory. Nikia asked her mother, "What does debonair mean?"

"It means...well, I'm not sure, I always thought it meant smart and sophisticated, charming."

Dan couldn't resist, "but it is also having a very strong faith in God and loving your neighbors as much as yourself. It's all about kindness, loving kindness. People who show loving kindness are debonair. Your mother--your mom is debonair."

Mildly protesting, Consuela confessed, "Thanks, but I have my moments."

"We all have our moments," Dan said.

Nikia looked at both of them. "I'm going to go for a swim," she said.

"The service isn't over," Daniel said, hoping they might talk some more.

"I'm going for a swim," Nikia repeated.

"Okay, dear," Consuela said.

Nikia was soon jumping off the diving board. The couple watched the rest of the service and joined in the last hymn.

As the organist played a Bach postlude, Dan and Consuela watched Nikia dive backward off the diving board.

"She's really good!" Dan said.

Consuela said, "She loves it. I hope she can be competitive."

"If she works at it-- and is debonair-- like you--"

"Ah. Maybe," Consuela answered.

Dan noticed she didn't return the compliment to him. Well, he wasn't very debonair.

He worried a lot. He wondered about Consuela. Would she continue to be debonair if they had to close a restaurant? Should they lay off a few more people now? Wait six more months and hope? The success of the restaurant was very important to Consuela, but so far she hadn't seemed as worried as he had been. His business was his life! It was who he was.

They could make it for six months. But what then? Given the international constraints of flying during the pandemic, how would Consuela feel if they had to cancel the trip they planned to see her family?

He didn't want to admit it but he liked Maria's sermon. Pastor Maria had pointed out that God loved the Pharisees. That was something he hadn't heard before. Maria had said the Pharisee was missing out because he wasn't asking God for help.

Dan had always thought of sin as stealing or committing murder or lying; that sort of thing was a sin. Not loving God and your neighbor as yourself--was *that* sin? Perhaps it was, but sin certainly would include murder and lying and which was not loving God or neighbor.

Thinking about the sermon, he couldn't help but ask himself, what should he, Dan, ask from God? How could he be more debonair?

Like the Pharisees, Dan prayed in church-- gave thanks, and prayed for the people suffering from the virus, and those who cared for them. He had prayed for Emma when she was so sick, but admittedly he had not prayed much since Emma died, which was a long time ago.

In fact, it had been years since he prayed for himself. Dan had been taught he was supposed to handle things, not need help. He figured God had plenty to do for people who needed help more than he did.

Perhaps he could ask God for help in making decisions or pray for an end to the virus. He could pray for his business to make it through COVID-19 successfully or if the worst happened, and he had to declare bankruptcy, he could ask for help in handling such a loss.

He no longer wanted to be like the Pharisees. Dan could give thanks right now! He was thankful for the customers who still came to their restaurants and those who ordered food online.

He could give thanks to Consuela and ask for help in being a good husband and to be a good stepfather for Nikia.

Yes, he needed help in having more understanding. Teenage years were tough--on parents.

Loving kindness. That was what it came down to--loving kindness.

If sin was a matter of not loving your neighbor and yourself equally, then everyone, including himself, was a sinner. Maybe, just maybe he would try to pray like the publican, "God be merciful to me, a sinner."

But first, he would go for a swim.

CHAPTER 2

The Parable of the Sower
Mike Reynolds and his sister, Gloria

Mike Reynolds was lighting a single candle on the coffee table when his sister Gloria came into the living room with a package of pastry in hand.

"Morning!" she said. "I brought you some coffee cake. Bought it yesterday, but it should still be fresh."

"I'm sure it will be fine!" Mike said, reaching for the cup of coffee on the table. "Glad you could come over this morning. I just launched Zoom."

"I'd like to come more often, but--"

"No worries," Mike said. "I don't expect you to come every Sunday. Sit down. We're in the waiting room."

"I'll put the coffee cake in the kitchen for later. I wanted to get here on time."

"You're fine," Mike said, looking at the screen. "Glad to have you here, Sis. I don't want to take you away from your family."

"Mike, I'm glad to get away! Before Covid, I made the kids go to church. Now, I let them choose one Sunday a month to stay home-- and we have no more arguments. Now they don't even need to get dressed up. Next Sunday, I may bring them here with me."

"That would be great," Mike said as Gloria quickly set the coffee cake down in the kitchenette and returned to the living room and sat down.

"What about your husband?"

"Andy says he'll wait to start back to church when we can go there and enjoy it. Who knows when that will be? Sometimes he watches with me on Zoom, but I'll bet he won't watch when I'm gone.

"Oh!" she cried, looking at the image of the two of them, visible on the upper left corner of the computer screen. I look terrible."

"Relax," Mike said. "None of us look as good on Zoom as we do in person. Thanks for coming over." He gave her a big smile which showed his gratitude but also betrayed some loneliness.

"Good morning," came Pastor Maria's greeting from the computer screen. "It's good to see you! I wish we were all together, but it is wonderful to see all your faces.

"This morning, we will open our service with a beautiful hymn, 'Joyful, Joyful, We Adore Thee.' The words will be on the screen if you did not download them from the bulletin."

Thou are giving and forgiving, ever blessing,
ever blest, well-spring of the joy of living, ocean
depth of happy rest!
Thou our Father, Christ our brother, all who
live in love are Thine;
Teach us how to love each other, lift us to the
joy divine!

(Verse 4, Text: Henry van Dyke, Sung to Ludwig van Beethoven's famous melody)

From the sofa, Mike and Gloria joined the choir in singing. Mike had a smooth tenor voice which Gloria envied.

It was good to sing together again. The two sounded almost like they were part of the choir.

Pastor Maria stepped to the altar and read the gospel -- *Matthew 3.9:*

> *"And he told them many things in parables, saying: 'Listen! A sower went out to sow. And as he sowed, some seeds fell on the path, and the birds came and ate them up.*

> *"Other seeds fell on rocky ground, where they did not have much soil, and they sprang up quickly since they had no depth of soil. But when the sun rose, they were scorched; and since they had no root, they withered away.*

> *"Other seeds fell among thorns, and the thorns grew up and choked them.*

> *"Other seeds fell on good soil and brought forth grain, some a hundredfold, some sixty, some thirty. Let anyone with ears listen!'*

> *"The Word of the Lord. "*

> *"Thanks, Be to God," responded Mike and Gloria, along with other participants.*

> *"This is one of my favorite parables, especially at this time of the year. As many of you know, I love to garden.*

"I can't help but think the Parable of the Sower should be named the Parable of the Soil. The differences in the harvesting is not the sower's fault, nor is there anything wrong with the seeds that were used.

"The problem is the soil. In our story, Jesus is not emphasizing the sower, but rather his emphasis is on different kinds of soil.

"All soil is not alike. Some soil is hard, some is stony, some is thorny and some is excellent! All do not yield the same.

"Jesus emphasizes the importance of awareness in hearing. 'Listen!' he says-- twice he says 'Listen!' Pay attention! There is something important here for you to learn.

"Not all listeners are alike. Some who were present when Jesus told the story probably found the message meaningless. Their ears heard the words, but their minds were wandering in other directions.

"Some might have greeted the story scornfully.

"Some did not respond because like the hard soil, their hearts were hard. The soil was fertile. It had the same richness as the best soil, but it lacked one thing familiar to us here in the desert!
"It was so hard the sown seed simply lay upon the surface until the birds came and devoured it. The

soil had been hardened for a long time, which is often the case for a listener who is unresponsive.

"It is possible to destroy our own spiritual sensitivity.

"A person develops a deadly callousness through a long, conscious process of ignoring the truth and persistently refusing to put wisdom into practice.

"There were eager and enthusiastic listeners present who had a quick response. But they proved a disappointment to themselves as well as others. Most likely they quit as quickly as they began. Their response was emotionally superficial instead of what was true for them and personally needed. They listened to inclinations rather than to the voice of responsibility— the ability to respond.

"We also have some who heard and responded too quickly, giving up because the weeds with thorns also spang up and grew in the good soil!

"It is easy for us to allow good wheat to be crowded out by thorns that choke them.

"Jesus mentions several kinds of thorns—first there is worry.

"Remember from the Sermon of the Mount:

'Therefore, I tell you, do not worry about your life, what you will eat or what you will drink, or about

your body, what you will wear. Is not life more than food, and the body more than clothing? Matthew 6.25.'

"Another thorn that Jesus mentions is money. Money is not an evil itself, but we can easily allow it to become more important than anything else.

"A third thorn is pleasure, which can become the person's most important desire.

"No matter how innocent or good something may be in itself, it becomes a thorn if it crowds out something more important.

"Even good works can be thorns if we become so busy doing good that we neglect our homes and families.

"Experiencing COVID-19 has helped us see what is most important.

"I have taken a second, third and fourth look at what my priorities are. You probably have too. Many of us have awakened to new insights on what is most important in life and recognized what have become thorns in our lives.

"Thankfully, heartfelt listeners are seekers of truth. They hear the word with an open mind and put the messages into practice.

"They live up to the light they have, because doing so makes the light brighter; their lights do not fade into darkness.

"If we practice our faith, the light grows. Heartfelt listeners have staying qualities. It takes patience to raise a crop.

When I was a little girl, I planted a garden of gladiolus from some bulbs my father gave me. I watched them carefully, but it seemed like nothing was happening. After a few days, I dug them all up to see how they were doing.

"I do not recommend doing this.

"It takes time to grow a garden. It takes time to grow character.

"During this time of the pandemic, we hear competing messages, ranging from 'Always wear a mask in public' to 'You don't need to wear a mask.' From 'Send your children to the classroom' to 'Keep your children at home until you are sure it is safe for them to attend.'

"Listen carefully. Tune your hearts and minds to the truth. Look at the sources of contradictory messages. Examine the motivation. These are difficult times, and there are many unknowns.

"Throughout history the desert has been a place for meditation, for seeking and finding spiritual guidance.

"Jesus went into the desert to wrestle with thorns, temptations, and to receive revelations.

"May we use this time in the desert caused by the pandemic to find a deeper sense of who we are and what our major life purposes are, to examine our priorities, eliminate some of our thorns, and to know and practice the truth.

"Blessings on our journeys!

"May God be with us and guide us on our paths.

"Amen."

Michael was listening but also questioning. Keep your hearts and minds on the truth. Who knew what the truth was these days?

The only real truth he knew was the power of thorns, always present in the background, always waiting to stick him good.

Sometimes Michael saw roses, but beneath the roses was a patch of thorns beckoning him, thorns that could torment him, reducing him to a whimpering helpless wreck of a human being.

At least now he knew what to look for.

Michael had not stopped drinking, but he had managed and finally vowed to again and again, repeatedly stop smoking. After what he had been through during his last drinking bout, Michael never wanted to go through such pain and humiliation as repeatedly stopping and then starting again.

He no longer would misspend his life trying to satisfy a craving for alcohol. Michael had vowed to himself and to his friends at AA that if he ever started drinking again, he would drink as much as possible the rest of his life, literally to hell with it.

Sounded crazy, but so far the power of that vow, the possibility of continuing the rest of his life with no hope of retrieval was so frightening that he had remained sober for two years.

The threat he made to himself empowered him to go forward. It was along with this huge change, that he decided to move closer to his sister for family support.

Gloria had been a second mother to him, sometimes a first, and when he arrived in town only a year and a half ago, he had stayed with Andy and their 11-year-old twins, Charlie and Chelsea for a few months.

Now, Michael, a CPA, had his own apartment and a good job with H & R Block. One could depend on people always needing help with their taxes. Besides, it was interesting to learn about people's lives.

Gloria brought Michael with her to church shortly after he arrived in Albuquerque.

Since March, when so many restrictions came, they got together at least once a month to watch a church service on Zoom.

Michael had gone to his sister's home a couple of times for services but found it too chaotic. He'd rather go to "Zoom church" in his own home.

From the kitchenette, Gloria brought a tray with the coffee cake and fresh coffee. "What did you think of the sermon?" Gloria asked.

"I thought it was right on," Michael said, "but unfortunately, people often don't recognize the thorns in their lives until it is too late. The damn thorns almost killed me. There are people watching this today, who need to see what their thorns are costing them. "

Gloria stared at him. "Do you think Pastor Maria was talking about addictions?"

"Yes, yes, I do. But I don't want to talk about me. Thanks to you and AA, I'm doing okay! But we all have our thorns, at least most of us. There are all kinds of addictions."

Gloria was quiet for a moment. "Well," she said, "Andy is so taken with his business, that except for football, it is all he thinks about. Now it looks like there may not be much football, not even college football, or the NFL. Andy's thorns are football and his business that gives life purpose. I don't know if that's so bad, but sometimes it feels like he hardly has time for us, or the church or God or anything else.

"Our kids? Well, Chelsea worries about not having friends; she is so shy. And Charlie seems too sensitive; he is too darn emotional, but at least he likes to play soccer. I worry about my kids. And I worry about you. I really do."

"You're always worrying, Gloria. Please, you don't need to worry about me. Maybe in some ways, I sort of like it. But I am Michael; I am responsible for Michael!"

"I worry that you can't go to AA meetings anymore. Those meetings are important," Gloria said. "Do you go to meetings on Zoom? I would think you need to be there in person."

"Zoom is better than nothing. I talk to my sponsor at least once a week; he helps me a lot.

"Alcoholics have a big problem with COVID-19. Having to stay home all the time has made alcoholism a bigger problem than ever. People are under a lot more stress; many have lost their jobs or are working too hard. None of us are safe. I'm not either."

"You don't think you're safe?" Gloria asked, alarmed.

"The national organization has had to tap into their reserves; they are running a huge deficit. Fortunately, we have some reserves."

"I'd be glad to give a contribution, but you know how Andy is."

"AA can't accept it anyway."

"Why not?"

"The 7th tradition."

"What's that?" Gloria asked.

"The 7th tradition means we take care of ourselves. While I appreciate your help, I don't want you to take care of me."

But a moment later he added, "I would like a piece of coffee cake."

"Good! More coffee?" Gloria got up and went back into the kitchenette where she poured two cups of coffee and sliced the pastry so each of them could have another piece.

Returning to the living room she watched as Michael took each bite. "Were you asking for a donation, Michael?"

"No, I explained the 7th tradition. You can't give to AA unless you are an alcoholic, and you're not. You're just a worrier."

"Do you like the coffee cake I brought?" she asked.
"It's fine, Gloria," he said, "and even if it didn't taste as good as it does, it would be okay."

"And why would that be?" she asked.

"Because you brought it to me."

"Well, maybe then I'll bring you more!"

"That would be good." He looked at her. "Sis, I do need to take care of myself."

"Well, I don't see what's the big deal about bringing a little coffee cake over."

"It's not," Mike agreed. "It's just that I don't want you to be so... so...intense about it. I'm fine. You're fine. The coffee cake is fine."

"So, what's the matter?"

"Well, just please don't worry so much...about me...about the kids...or Andy for that matter. You're like our mom."

"No, I'm not!" Gloria said. "Mom was always feeling sorry for herself. I don't do that!"

"I'm sorry, Gloria. You're right. You are *not* like Mom. You don't feel sorry for yourself the way she sometimes did, which made me crazy. But you do worry too much."

"I'm going to take the damn coffee cake home and never bring another piece!" she said.

Mike laughed but backtracked. "Please don't do that," he said, "I promise to be more grateful. You are my sister. I love you!"

For a minute, they sat silently.

"Okay," Gloria said. "Okay. I'll still bring you a coffee cake. I love you too."

Mike wasn't finished. "Do you remember Maria's sermon, the part about not worrying? Isn't life more important than coffee cake, the body's health more important than clothes?"

Gloria giggled. "Does my worrying, my thorns, bother you?"

"Well, actually it doesn't bother me much, but it hurts you."

"Don't you worry?" she asked.

"Of course, I worry. I worry about some of my clients. I worry about not having... a partner... and I worry most about what happens if I should... (he hardly dared say the words) ...not remain sober. But I don't worry as much as I once did."

"Well, that's good!" Goria said. "Mike, I know I worry too much. I probably inherited it."

"That's not a good reason. That's an excuse," Mike said.

"You're right. You are right!"

"Enjoy life! Enjoy living! That's what it's all about."

"And...I...I.. I need to let go of worrying. But you of all people! My little brother is giving me advice."

"Getting rid of thorns is like weeds. Nip them early. Don't let them grow or they will take over. Change your thoughts and feelings to how glad you are to be alive. Be grateful for what you have in life. You..you can stop them in their tracks. If you let weeds or worries grow, they take over. I know."

"All right. I'll try," Gloria said. "I'll give it a good try."
They sat quietly together for a few more minutes. Gloria finally got up to leave.

"One more piece of coffee cake?" Michael asked.

"Well, I'm not sure," Gloria said. "I was sort of thinking of taking the rest home."

Michael, surprised, looked up at her.

"Just kidding!" she said, smiling. "Just practicing really. Take some, little brother!"

CHAPTER 3

The Merciful Samaritan
Rita and Carl Allman

Rita and Carl sat watching and listening on YouTube to Pastor Maria as she opened the church service with a few announcements:

'We need volunteers to help staff the Community Food Bank this Thursday. Please contact the office if you are available and wish to help.

Oh, I would love to help, Rita thought. *I have hardly been out of the house.*

Rita was tired of sitting at home, rarely going anywhere. How she wanted to be of use! If she could help at the Community Food Bank, she could get her mind off her problems.

Rita glanced at Carl, afraid he would make a fuss and expect her not to help out at the food bank. But apparently, he hadn't been paying attention, because he didn't look at her. Well, she would talk to him later when he was in a good mood. Unfortunately, Carl was hardly ever in a good mood these days. COVID-19 had been hard enough, but the last two months had been miserable for both Rita and Carl.

For more than two months there had been no communication between them and their only child, Leah. It was hard on Rita who for years had always talked at least weekly with her daughter, and it was even harder on Carl who liked to joke with Leah. Rita was afraid they would never be happy again. Leah would soon be getting her Ph.D.

Carl was waiting for Leah to come to her senses, but Rita knew better. Leah was like her father. She was going to marry whomever she chose, and she had chosen Haim. Yesterday a friend of Leah's had told Rita that Leah and Haim were planning to be married this fall! Their only child! Leah was making plans without including them. Rita just couldn't tell Carl. They had heard nothing about their plans.

So much to worry about. What kind of wedding was Leah planning? They had to be part of it! Wasn't she going to even invite them?? What was Haim's family like? Where did they plan to live? Did either Leah or Haim have job offers? Did they plan to have children? When was Leah going to contact them?

She had to stop thinking about it! Worrying didn't help! Rita turned her attention to Pastor Maria opening the service liturgy, "The Lord be with you--".

"And also with you," Rita and Carl responded.

"Let us join together in reading the prayer of the day."

The words of the prayer appeared on the screen: "God of Hope, show us how to live as your children, as sisters and brothers on our blessed earth..." Pastor Maria began.

"The word of our Lord." Pastor Maria said, at the prayers' end.

"Thanks be to God," the muted listeners responded.

The opening hymn was Rita's favorite, *"Toma, oh Dios, mi volhuntad,"* the Spanish musical version of "Take My

Life and Let it Be," with its strong rhumba beat, played with strong bongo drum accents by the church praise band.

(Text: Frances Havergal, Spanish text: Vicente Mendoza)

Rita would have loved to sing it in Spanish, but today she sang in English, so her words were the same as others in the virtual congregation.

Rita's mind wandered until she was suddenly brought back to the present time by Pastor Maria who was at the podium beginning her sermon:

"Our parable today is The Merciful Samaritan, often referred to as 'The Good Samaritan.'

"The word "good" has such a wide array of meanings—generous, skilled, well-behaved. In order to be more specific, we will refer to the main character as "The Merciful Samaritan. "

"The story begins with a lawyer heckling Jesus by asking a question, not because he doesn't know the answer, but with the hope that Jesus' answer will get him in trouble with the authorities.

"Jesus often took such occasions as an opportunity to teach an important lesson. That is exactly what he does in today's lesson from Luke, Chapter 10, Vs 25-37:

"Just then a lawyer stood up to test Jesus. 'Teacher,' he said, 'what must I do to inherit eternal life?'

"He said to him, 'What is written in the law? What do you read there?'

"He answered, 'You shall love the Lord your God with all your heart, and with all your soul, and with all your strength, and with all your mind; and your neighbor as yourself.'

"And he said to him, 'You have given the right answer; do this, and you will live.'

"But wanting to justify himself, he asked Jesus, 'And who is my neighbor?'"

"Jesus replied, 'A man was going down from Jerusalem to Jericho, and fell into the hands of robbers who stripped him, beat him, and went away leaving him half dead. Now by chance, a priest was going down that road; and when he saw him, he passed by on the other side. So likewise, a Levite, when he came to the place and saw him, passed by on the other side. But a Samaritan while traveling came near him; and when he saw him, he was moved with pity. He went to him and bandaged his wounds, having poured oil and wine on them. Then he put him on his own animal, brought him to an inn, and took care of him. The next day he took out two denari, gave them to the innkeeper, and said, 'Take care of him; and when I come back, I will repay you whatever more you spend.'

"Which of these three, do you think, was a neighbor to the man who fell into the hands of the robbers?"

"He said, 'The one who showed him mercy.'

"Jesus said to him, 'Go and do likewise.'"

"The word of our Lord."

"Thanks be to God," responded the congregation.

Pastor Maria proceeded with her sermon:

"At this time in history with COVID-19 causing so much suffering and death, human kindness is more necessary than ever. Acts of kindness now mean more than we can imagine. It means everything.

"The story of the merciful Samaritan is a familiar story to us. It is the story of someone from a different ethnic group, who helps a stranger, who is not from his ethnic group. It is a difficult situation where providing help is inconvenient and costly. The kindness provided is amazing! Let's take it from the top:

"An ordinary man, not anyone in particular, is robbed, beaten and left to suffer and die along the roadside.

"First a pillar in God's temple, the priest, comes by. He passes on the other side. We can't help but sympathize a bit with the priest. Would we do any different? Then a Levite passes by. A Levite is someone who belonged to the order that the choir members were chosen from. Both men appear indifferent to human suffering in spite of their religious connections.

"And then comes the merciful Samaritan, a person from an ethnic group at great odds with the Jewish community.

"The Samaritan feels sorry for the man in the ditch. He gets off his donkey to help the man. After applying oil and wine to the man's wounds, he bandages him up, puts the man on his donkey and arranges for him to be taken care of at an inn. The Samaritan gives the innkeeper two denari and promises to pay any further charges if necessary. He has assumed responsibility; the others have not.

"Jesus asks, which one of the three people, who saw the man who was hurt, is the good neighbor?

"The lawyer answers correctly, 'the Merciful Samaritan.' The one who helped. Kindness. Helpfulness. Responsibility. We are to do likewise. We are to be kind, even merciful—not just to people who are like us, but to all human beings.

"Jesus is not setting up a rule by which we can obtain eternal life, but the destiny of eternal life is determined by the quality of the life we live here and now, our actions, and how we treat other people.

"We do not win eternal life by doing good, but we do not inherit life without doing good. Something is radically wrong with a person who belongs to the Christian church if he or she lacks human kindness.

"Through expressions of kindness and mercy, we can make it easier for our neighbors to live good lives; together, we have the power to greatly improve and strengthen life in our communities.

"Human kindness offered within the spirit of God is a gracious, exciting, meaningful way of life; it is the true test of the religious spirit.

"Unfortunately, kindness can be abused when it has a false face hiding selfish motives, or when it is used to weaken people instead of helping them. Such acts are not matters of kindness!

"There are some people who might say that what happened to the traveler who was robbed and beaten was his own fault. He should have known better, maybe taken a different route.

"However, all of us are vulnerable to thieves. We all make mistakes. And even if a person has contributed to the problems he or she has, the need is there to be handled whatever the situation or causes.

"The best response is always a kind response. Kindness cost the merciful Samaritan time and money. But the need was met; the problem was solved.

"This morning, I would like to conclude with another short story, another parable you may not have heard of. It is called Genesis 51. Often we read from the Old Testament as well as the New Testament on Sunday morning; usually the older text is read first.

"This morning, I am going to do what seems like the opposite.

"If you look it up in your Bible, it will be evident that Genesis ends with Chapter 50.

"Genesis, Chapter 51 is not part of the Bible. It is not a fraud nor is it meant to be deceptive. It is simply a creative story! Genesis, Chapter 51 was written by Benjamin Franklin while he was living in England.

"Franklin enjoyed imitating the Biblical language. He sometimes read Chapter 51 aloud to friends who visited him as entertainment, some of whom said they did not recall such a chapter in the Bible.

"Franklin's story was written for reasons which are not only creative but also meaningful. First, it serves as a creative reinforcement of the story of The Merciful Samaritan. It shows kindness, helpfulness, and hospitality to people different from us.

"And it was written by a founder of our country, Benjamin Franklin, who signed both the Declaration of Independence and our Constitution. From a forefather, Benjamin Franklin, we have a message for our time, one all of us need to hear.

"Benjamin Franklin especially enjoyed using old Biblical language for effect. He delighted in reading Genesis 51, to visitors:"

"And it came to pass, that Abraham sat in the door of his tent, about the going down of the sun. And behold a man, bowed with age, came from the wilderness leaning on a staff. And Abraham arose and met him, and said unto him, 'Turn in, I pray thee, and wash thy feet, and tarry all night, and thou shalt arise early on the morrow, and go thy way.' But the man said, 'Nay, for I will abide under this tree.'

"And Abraham pressed him greatly; so he turned, and they went into the tent, and Abraham baked unleavened bread, and they did eat.

"And when Abraham saw that the man blessed not God, he said unto him, 'Wherefore does thou not worship the most high God, Creator of heaven and earth?'

"And the man answered and said, 'I do not worship the God thou speakest of, neither do I call upon his name; for I have made to myself a God which abideth always in my house and provideth me with all things.'

"And Abraham's zeal was kindled against the man, and he arose and drove him forth with blows into the wilderness. And at midnight God called unto Abraham, saying, Abraham, where is the stranger?

"And Abraham answered and said, 'Lord, he would not worship Thee, neither would he call upon Thy name, therefore have I driven him out from before my face into the wilderness.'

"And God said, 'Have I not borne with him these hundred and ninety and eight years, and nourished him, and clothed him, notwithstanding his rebellion against me, and couldst not thou, that art thyself a sinner, bear with him one night?'

"And Abraham said. 'Let not the anger of my Lord wax against His servant; lo! I have sinned, forgive me, I pray thee.'

"And Abraham arose and went forth into the wilderness, and sought diligently for the man, and found him and returned with him to the tent, and when he had entreated him kindly, he sent him away on the morrow."

"This story about Abraham shows us that we are to be kind to everyone without regard to where they come from, or their religious or political affiliations. Kindness is a form of mercy we need to practice every day of our lives.

"At this time in history with COVID-19 causing so much suffering and death of thousands and thousands of people we need kindness more than ever.

"Kindness is not something to take for granted. It means much more. Acts of kindness will get us through these difficult days."

Pastor Maria invited the congregation: "Let us pray...."

Rita admired the good Samaritan for helping the man who had been beaten and who obviously needed help but doing that sort of thing could be dangerous. She understood why people passed by him on the other side. She would have done the same, especially if she were alone. If she had someone with her, someone strong, they could probably help, but even that took courage.

Rita understood Abraham's reluctance to invite a person into his home, someone who prayed to a different God. That was difficult! She especially admired Abraham for going searching and finding that person. After making him leave, it must have been very awkward and difficult to invite him back into his home. No way could she have done that. No way.

Rita listened to the pastor's liturgical prayer and then added her own prayer silently.

Please God, Jesus, whoever is listening, show me, help me-- show me acts of kindness I can do. I want to help someone other than myself.

Instantly, an image of her prospective son-in-law Haim came into her mind. He was neither what she expected nor wanted. Rita had hoped she would be able to help by assisting with the food bank. Carl might accept her help there. She knew what to do, and they needed help. Food. People needed food!

But it was Haim whose image she saw. He wasn't smiling. He was standing there looking just like he had on that horrible evening when Leah brought him home from graduate school and introduced him.

Why hadn't Leah prepared them? Didn't she understand how Carl felt about his only child, how much she meant to them? How much they loved her!

Leah hadn't told them about Hiam's religion before their visit! And she certainly hadn't talked about marriage. Leah had simply told her parents that Haim was a fellow student at the University graduate school. Then, together, on their visit unexpectedly they announced their engagement!

Carl hadn't said anything disapproving that night, or the next day. Everyone was pleasant, but obviously, there was a lot of tension. You could cut it with a dull knife.

Rita understood why Carl felt it was necessary for him to intervene; he felt he had to prevent his daughter from ruining her life. But unfortunately, he let his emotions get in his way. Leah was lovely and talented. Soon she would have her Ph.D. He didn't want their only daughter to marry a Muslim; he believed it would make their life difficult and hurt her career. He didn't see how it could work out. Carl realized Leah would be upset with him for interfering, but surely, she would get over it.

Carl wasn't being his usual self. He wasn't being kind. Especially when he made that fateful telephone call. If only Carl had not telephoned Leah as soon as she returned to school and told her exactly how he felt.

Rita didn't want their friends to know what happened. She wished she could support her daughter, but her husband needed her support too.

It had all happened too fast.

Leah had said, "Dad, don't be so prejudiced. Haim is a good person. I love him. You'll get to like him too. He isn't that different from us... Muslims accept Jesus."

"Oh really, well what about Mohammed?"

"They just see Mohammed as the greatest prophet."

"Well, I sure as hell don't. Honey, I understand you love him now. But marriage isn't easy and life doesn't get any easier. You'll be sorry if you do this. It will be the mistake of your life." Leah responded, "I'm sorry Daddy. You're wrong. You're just plain wrong."

Ever since that fateful call, it seemed too difficult to mend the hurt between father and daughter, impossible to bridge their differences. But Rita would never stop trying.

Now, as the sermon ended, Rita reached over to hold Carl's hand. He looked down at their entwined hands, then gazed up at her with a sad but knowing smile. Carl was not stupid. He also had been listening to Pastor Maria; he had lost the battle, but his eyes were hopeful. Losing the battle was necessary. It was his best option, and he knew it. He prayed for the ability to accept the marriage his daughter wanted.

Rita squeezed Carl's hand to say, *it is going to be alright. We love each other. I'm here for you.* Carl managed to smile.

They would make it alright and learn a lot in the process. Pastor Maria: "For our closing hymn we shall sing "Canticle of the Turning," Hymn 723. The lyrics will be on the screen.

Together Carl and Rita joined in the chorus of each verse:

My heart shall sing of the day you bring.
Let the fires of your justice burn.
Wipe away all tears, for the dawn
draws near,
And the world is about to turn.
(text: Rory Cooney)

CHAPTER 4

New Patches on Old Garments
Sue Ellen, Jack and Stacey

Little Stacey sat at her very own desk carefully selecting her next crayon. Her limited work area was covered by numerous, colorful crayons. Some were broken, a few still unused in the box, along with two coloring books and numerous "connect the dots" worksheets.

Nearby, her mother, Sue Ellen, sat on the sofa in their apartment living room watching and listening to Pastor Maria begin her sermon via Zoom.

"The Parable of New Patches on Old Garments," Pastor Maria began. "I will read a one-sentence parable from Matthew 9:16:

"No one sews a piece of unshrunk cloth on an old cloak, for the patch pulls away from the cloak, and a worse tear is made...

"Today is a historic day," Pastor Maria said, looking directly into the camera. "Seventy-five years ago, on Sunday morning, August 6, 1945, the Japanese radar system reported the approach of enemy planes.

"At 8 o'clock a.m. that day it was determined there were only three planes and the alert was removed; 10 minutes later, the atomic bomb was dropped on Hiroshima.

"*Immediately, Japan's national broadcasting company realized that the Hiroshima radio had left the air. Attempts were made to reach the station by telephone, but no one answered.*

"*They tried to reach the city by telegraph, but the lines had been cut.*

"*The government officials were very concerned; they had also tried to contact the city. Finally, the army sent a colonel to Hiroshima in an airplane.*

"*One hundred miles from the city, the colonel looked down and saw a huge pillar of smoke stretching extraordinarily high into the sky. He circled the city in the plane. When he looked down, to his utter amazement, he saw that more than 60% of Hiroshima had been completely destroyed.*

"*It had all happened in a few seconds. The atom bomb dropped on the city of 343,000 people exploded with the power of 20 thousand tons of TNT. The bomb killed 600 of the 800 firemen, 260 of the 300 physicians and surgeons, and 800 of 2400 nurses. More than 100,000 people were killed and more than 100,000 were injured, many of whom died later from burns, radiation or shock.*

"*This is a terribly heavy burden for Americans to confront. The United States of America, our own beloved country, was the first nation to cause such sudden destruction and death.*

"We can find excuses—such as the attack on Pearl Harbor and shortening the war to save lives for both Americans and Japanese--but it is difficult, if not impossible, to justify.

"In 1946 The Federal Council of Churches made the following statement: 'The surprise bombing of Hiroshima and Nagasaki are morally indefensible.'

"It is a clear and correct assessment.

"What will happen if another nation initiates an atomic attack on us? We are not in a defensible place to pass judgment on such an action.

"The atomic bomb that fell on Hiroshima on Sunday morning seventy-five years ago was a pitiful, small toy compared to the bombs we have today. The state of the world has been and remains a serious matter of concern throughout history.

"What can we do? What can we do to preserve the earth on which we live?

"In the little parable of the new patch on an old garment, Jesus suggests a principle by which we can begin to find an answer.
"Jesus was accused of breaking Jewish laws which would make their lives difficult. He answered their concerns by telling this parable. He is challenging

them to leave the barren past and enter into a new and better life.

"The old ways, the current ways of living are insufficient. They are as old and worn out as an old garment that must be laid aside. Putting new patches on an old garment only makes things worse. It is useless for us to try and patch it up.

"Jesus was inviting his disciples, and he is inviting us to a new and different way of living.

"His image of the old garment and a new patch is a way of helping the disciples and it helps us understand that God has something better in store for us. A new patch does not help. It makes matters worse. Change is necessary.

"I believe our experience with COVID-19 is offering us the opportunity to make major changes.

"Change is needed, and change is resisted. People tend to want to keep the old ways and fight change.

"The first electric Remington typewriter came on the market in 1974. It was received with indifference and there were many arguments against it.

"We now have computers in virtually every aspect of our lives. In spite of the many problems computers cause, we are grateful for them, and we could not manage life without them.

"When James Simpson discovered the use of chloroform as an anesthetic, he first used it to ease women's suffering during childbirth. The church was against it, and some church leaders argued that 'God ordained women to suffer in childbirth.'

"What is true about new inventions is equally true when it involves religion or culture.

"Women finally received the right to vote 100 years ago, a change which created huge changes in society, but we cannot imagine changing it back!

"Today, COVID-19 has made it necessary to confront desperately needed changes we can no longer ignore. The world needs a whole new garment; a patch here, a patch there, will no longer do. We must change!

"COVID-19 has caused us to confront a number of critical problems: racism, poverty, disparity in income, lack of community, disregard for the health and welfare of others, and dangers occurring due to climate change. These areas and other crises have been exposed.

"We must confront the problems in our society which are not only harmful, but morally wrong, outmoded, and unsustainable.

"During this massive pandemic, we have realized how much we need and rely on one another, and how important our families, community, and *world are to all of us. The difficulties we are experiencing teach us to be more aware we are all interdependent.*

"We are more deeply grateful for each other, for people we do not know, people we cannot do without. We are more grateful for services we no longer can take for granted.

"We cannot just patch things up! We need to find new ways of living. We live in a complex, difficult time, and I believe we either chose or were chosen to be here.

"This is a time of enormous opportunity to create positive changes. We must use this time to assess our situation and chart new ways.

"With God's help, we can create a new world built on a foundation of love, deep gratitude, respect, and concern for all people.

"Let us pray the day will come when we can again worship together safely, when we can shake each other's hands, even hug one another.
"Do you remember what it was like? Do you realize how much we took for granted?

"There will be a Sunday morning when we will all sing together without masks, where there is no fear of spreading new germs, a time we can kneel together shoulder to shoulder in communion.

"We will again enjoy the simple pleasure of having coffee together.

"I don't know what it will be like when this pandemic retreats into history, but I know we will be changed. We will discover new ways of helping each other and new ways of serving. We are not going to come out of this crisis with only simple patches. New garments must be created!

"Let us use our time in the desert to learn how to live in faith and love, caring for one another, caring for our earth, caring for our families, community, church, country, world, blessed by deeper understanding, and gratitude and affection for life itself.

"A new day is coming! What a joyful time it will be!

"Amen."

Disturbed by Pastor Maria's message, Sue Ellen decided to leave the service. She didn't even need to bid goodbye on "chat," which was something she liked about Zoom. She could leave the service indiscreetly without being noticed.

For several moments Sue sat staring at the empty computer screen and then went to get a second cup of coffee. Sue sat down again to think things over. The tone and the content of Pastor Maria's message bothered Sue Ellen. She had never heard her pastor speak so negatively and with such seriousness about the future. Sue Ellen was waiting for things to return to normal. Could the coming years be very difficult for everyone?

What if the economy did not recover? What if heat waves, fires, earthquakes, tornadoes and hurricanes got worse? What if the virus continued to kill people around the world or some other even worse strain of the disease spread? What if Russia, China, or Iran started another war? What if the country's racial problems didn't get resolved and political divisions became even worse? What kind of future would Stacey have?

"My color broke," Stacey complained.

"Well, take another crayon," Sue Ellen offered

"I don't have any more blue ones," Stacey wailed. Sue Ellen got up from the sofa found a teal-colored crayon in the box and handed it to Stacey.

"That's not blue!" Stacey said tearfully.

"It is sort of blue." her mother assured her. "It is the best we can do right now. We'll get some new crayons tomorrow." Stacey swallowed her tears, took the crayon reluctantly, and soon was coloring again. Sue Ellen went back to her worrying.

From the way Pastor Maria had spoken, huge, big changes were needed. She seemed to suggest that such changes were already happening, brought on by responses to COVID-19. The most important change was for people to care for each other more, love each other more, and love themselves more.

True there were stories of people sacrificing to help one another, but the newspapers were crowded with more stories of violence and dissension.

Sue Ellen wondered; *Have I been living in too small a world?* It did seem she had been focusing too much, almost completely-- on her and Jack's wedding. Sue Ellen knew why their wedding meant so much to her. She had not had a church ceremony for her first wedding; they had rushed into marriage because she was pregnant.

The marriage had lasted only a year and while she regretted her decision to marry her first husband, Doug, Sue Ellen was very grateful for Stacey.

As for Doug, she was still working on forgiving him and for forgiving herself for being so gullible. He had seemed so wonderful, so genuine. According to her therapist, he was a sociopath which explained his lies, secret girlfriends, and overspending. Sue Ellen was well over Doug.

Stacey! Stacey! Stacey! Sue Ellen couldn't imagine life without her. Stacey had given her a reason to live, a reason to stay sane and Sue Ellen worked hard to be the best mother she could be. Now that Jack was in their lives, they would be a real family which was much more important than the wedding. Having a big wedding was going to have been Sue's announcement to the world-- everything was alright. But everything in the world was not alright. A lot of things were all wrong.

Sue Ellen's wedding was not the only event in the world that had been affected by the pandemic. She had been so focused on postponing their wedding that she had not realized how COVID-19 was affecting the rest of the world. People had really suffered; many had died. She and Jack had merely postponed their wedding.

Now, as she sat in her living room, Sue Ellen allowed herself to imagine for one last time, the wedding they had planned as if it were a memory rather than an event that had never happened: She imagined Stacey, her flower girl daughter, adorable with her long brown ringlets, smiling confidently in a lemon-yellow tulle gown, throwing pink rose petals on the carpet. She imagined Sue Ellen's best friend and her sister preceding her down the aisle in their fuchsia bridesmaid gowns.

Everyone stood as Sue Ellen, radiant in her white strapless wedding gown, walked gracefully down the aisle with her father. Jack's groomsmen, his two brothers, looked very serious as she approached them, but Jack grinned at her as he reeled her in like she was the catch of his lifetime. The entire "picture show" traveled in a perfect vision of her imagination: the church pipe organ played "*Jesu, Joy of Man Desiring.*"

It all was so perfect.

It was so unfair.

It was also unreal.

And it was past tense.

It was all so over!

Months ago, Jack and Sue Ellen had sent out "Save the Date" postcards with a romantic picture of her and Jack on the front. Two weeks later they had sent out a new version of the postcard: "Change of Plans! Wedding postponed due to COVID-19."

Yes, Jack and Sue Ellen's wedding was one of hundreds of New Mexico events delayed until a future date. And now, for the first time, it didn't seem nearly as consequential to Sue Ellen as it had before she heard Pastor Maria's sermon. They had canceled reservations for their honeymoon in Hawaii, a spectacular wedding cake, and a once popular band, whose members were suddenly unemployed. At least Sue Ellen and Jack had safe jobs. Her job as a research assistant at Sandia Labs and Jack's job as a hospital administrator was still viable, but who knew what the future would bring?

Sue Ellen no longer wanted to wait any longer. She wanted to marry Jack as soon as possible! Putting patches on old garments was not what should happen! It was not that her new wedding dress was old or that not having a big wedding would change the world.

It was simply that time was moving on. Waiting for the wedding she dreamed of had suddenly seemed-- not smart, but gauche; it was like insisting on wearing a gown that no longer fit time, place, or her own style; it was like wearing a sundress to work on the coldest day of the year.

She would talk to Jack. Maybe they could do something completely different, something brand new. She couldn't wait to talk to him, tell him how much she loved him, how she didn't want to wait for the damn virus to be over. What would Jack want? What would he now consider to be their ideal wedding?

Later that night, after Stacey was asleep, Sue Ellen and Jack sat in the living room to talk things over:

She: I've been thinking that maybe we shouldn't wait any longer. What if...what if we got married now-- quickly-- what would you like our wedding to be like, given the virus and all that is happening?

He: Really? You mean it-- You really mean it? Let me see.... I would like-- I would like us to go for a walk in the woods-- in the bosque-- early in the morning, just as the sun comes up-- you and I -- and Stacey and Pastor Maria of course, and well, also your sister and your best friend, and my brothers. We'll just go walking until we come to the perfect place. And when we find it, when you and I agree that this is the place to get married, we stop and say our vows.

She: Okay...Okay! What will you wear? Your tux?

He: Nope, everyone wears jeans. Well, okay, we can wear our tuxes. They are western tuxedos.

She: I like it! I really do! Then I could wear my wedding dress! I'll have it shortened, but I can't wear high heels in the woods. Cowboy boots! I'll get some white boots! Maybe with some rhinestones? What about our parents? We have to invite my mom and dad. They would kill me if we didn't invite them. And your parents. Could your Mom go down the trail in a wheelchair?

He: We'll explain the risks to them. I think they'll be able to come. I think they'll understand.

She: Okay. If they understand.

He: We'll get boots for Stacey.

She: Oh, she would love that! Stacey would love that.

He: We will need to socially distance our guests from each other.

She: What about flowers?

He: Roses, not a lot of them. But only red roses!

She: And can we have a photographer?

He: Nope, absolutely not!

She: (disappointed) Oh.

He: Just kidding! I know how important it is to you. I know someone who could do it. Maybe we can even do a video, and everyone could see our wedding later--maybe at our 25th-anniversary party?

She: Great idea! Or maybe... We *could* have a postponed reception or a *first-anniversary* party. Oh, Jack! I love it! I love you!

And so, it was.

CHAPTER 5

The Ten Lepers
Alicia, Ricardo and Becky, Ian

October 18, Sunday

From The Albuquerque Journal:

Virus spike strains New Mexico hospitals. This time shortage of medical staff, not PPE, is the key concern. Of primary concern is a shortage of nurses, doctors and respiratory therapists. Yesterday there was a record high of 819 new cases. The age group 65 and over has the highest case count on record; more deaths are expected due to the major increase in this age group.

Meanwhile, at Becky and Ricardo's home:

Alicia's family--daughter Becky, son-in-law Ricardo, and 7-year-old grandson, Ian-- were all in their places in front of a large computer screen, ready for Sunday church services via Zoom.

"May I have some crackers?" Ian asked.

"How do you ask?" Alicia reminded him.

"May I please have some crackers, Grandma?"

"No, but you can have some pretzels," Alicia's daughter, Becky answered. "The crackers are for communion." A table in front of the large TV featured two lighted candles, three half-filled shot glasses of red wine, a wooden bowl of pretzels, and a small plate of wheat crackers.

"Okay," Ian said.

He was at his small desk covered with an array of Legos and a tablet of drawing paper. Ian stopped building his Lego village to get up and help himself to pretzels. He glanced over at his grandmother for a moment.

Alicia, recently widowed, smiled at Ian, her treasured grandchild who was named after her husband. How Alicia enjoyed these Sunday mornings! The ease of not having to dress up, drive several miles, park the car, and arrive at church in time made Sundays more relaxing. No reason to dress up. Alicia had not worn a dress for months and she no longer hurried around on Sunday mornings.

Nevertheless, in spite of the ease and convenience of staying home, she missed going to "real church." Alicia missed passing the peace and the feeling of oneness when kneeling with others. She missed having coffee afterward and talking to real, live people.

Would this pandemic ever end? Would they all be able to go back and live normally some day?

Most of all, Alicia missed the choir. She had joined the choir less than a year ago, shortly after arriving in Albuquerque. After singing for only a few weeks, and just as she was getting to know other choir members, the virus ruined everyone's plans!

Without warning, the church was closed. The choir was "over" before Easter arrived! There was no opportunity to sing the music they had so carefully rehearsed, or even say goodbye to one another and wish each other good luck for an unforeseeable future.

"It's starting, Grandma!" Ian announced as Pastor Maria appeared on the screen. She welcomed everyone and announced the opening hymn, "Now Thank we all our God," page 839. "Please sing along with the choir members on screen but keep your microphones mute so the sound doesn't become distorted."

The family watched a video performance of a half dozen non-high-risk choir members standing 10 feet apart. Most were wearing cut-off shorts and singing through masks. Who had ever expected that singing could be dangerous?

Becky had prepared two copies of the bulletin with the hymn verses printed on them; she gave one copy to her mother. She and Ricardo shared the other copy.

Alicia enjoyed hearing her son-in-law sing. Ricardo had a beautiful bass voice and Alicia enjoyed singing along with Ricardo and Becky.

Choir members and organ music sent electronic waves into 47 homes across Albuquerque and beyond:

Now thank all our God with hearts and hands and voices.

Who wondrous things have done, in whom the world rejoices.

Who from our mothers' arms has blessed us on our way with countless gifts of love and still is our today."

(Text: Martin Rinkhart, tr. Catherine Winkworth)

Following the hymn, the camera focused on Pastor Maria opening a Bible and announcing the text: *"The Ten Lepers, Luke 17.11-19:*

"Now on his way to Jerusalem, Jesus traveled along the border between Samaria and Galilee. As he was going into a village, ten men who had leprosy met him. They stood at a distance and called out in a loud voice, "Jesus, Master, have pity on us!"

"When he saw them, he said, 'Go, show yourselves to the priests.' And as they went, they were cleansed.

"One of them, when he saw he was healed, came back, praising God in a loud voice. He threw himself at Jesus' feet and thanked him—and he was a Samaritan. Jesus asked, 'Were not all ten cleansed? Where are the other nine? Has no one returned to give praise to God except this foreigner?'

"Then he said to him, 'Rise and go; your faith has made you well.'

"The word of our Lord," Pastor Maria concluded.

"Thanks be to God," responded Alicia, Ricardo and Becky. Pastor Maria looked out at the virtual congregation and began her sermon:

"This morning, I invite you to go on a trip with me to Hawaii. "Whenever I think of the Parable of the

Ten Lepers, I remember Kalaupapa which is in one of the most remote places on earth; it is located on the island of Molokai where there still exists the remnants of a leper colony.

"The colony is located at the foot of cliffs reaching 3000 feet above sea level, some of the highest cliffs in the world. When I visited there in 2015, there were still six lepers living in the village.

"The colony was established in 1866 because of an isolation law enacted by King Kamehameha V. The law, which remained in effect for 103 years, sent 8,000 lepers into exile to be quarantined in Kalaupapa, usually for the rest of their lives. When the isolation was lifted in 1969, those who had grown up there did not want to return to society.

"When the outbreak of leprosy occurred in the 1800s, the Hawaiians were desperate. They had no immunity to the disease and no treatment for this deadly, disfiguring, highly contagious illness.

"When it was learned that someone had leprosy, now called Hansen's disease, children as well as adults were sent immediately to Molokai, never to see their families again. Some patients were thrown overboard when their ship brought them within two miles of the shore; it was up to them to swim to the island in order to survive.
"For 25 years Father Damian, the pastor and physician on the island, cared for the lepers before he died from the disease.

"Until I went to the Island, I had not heard of Sister Marianne, an American Franciscan nun from Syracuse, NY, who was born in Germany.

"She is deeply loved by the Hawaiian people, not only for the medical care she gave the patients, but for the humanitarian way of life she brought to the island for 35 years. Sister Marianne made life enjoyable for patients quarantined there.

"She enabled them to participate in activities like gardening as well as become involved in musical and other artistic pursuits to develop their talents. She encouraged them to play games, to laugh and learn as well as receive medical care.

"Many lepers who came to the island married, but their children were removed soon after they were born in order to live in a safe environment. The severe quarantine seems cruel and inhumane but by isolating the Lepers, thousands of lives were saved.

"Today we too are coping with an infectious pandemic, but one with major differences. Leprosy is caused by a bacteria; COVID-19 is a virus.

"Also, today we have better ways of treating infectious diseases. We have ventilators.

"Patients brought to the island sometimes had to swim two miles to shore to survive! I would not have made it! Today, we also have Zoom and other technology that makes communication possible on a regular basis, even allowing us to have church services such as this one.

"To prevent the spread of the Covid virus, we wear masks, wash our hands and stay home as much as possible. There are also similarities between leprosy then and COVID-19 now. We too isolate patients and quarantine those affected. Like Sister Marianne and Father Damian, today's caretakers of those who have the virus put their lives on the line just as doctors and nurses did for the leprosy patients at Kalaupapa.

"Today, we pray for all who are suffering from COVID-19 just as Hawaiians prayed for those suffering from leprosy. Our experience with COVID-19, even though different from Leprosy, gives us a sense of how the lepers and their families must have felt. We understand how painful it is to be infectious, dangerously ill and separated from all you hold dear.

"We already mourn the loss of almost 200,000 lives in just the last six months. Hundreds of thousands more may die from this disease before we have a vaccine. While there are many who have few symptoms and only mild cases, thousands of people are struggling. Many of them are dying.

"The ten lepers in the parable were all facing the same possibility--a difficult death. There was no cure and no vaccination, but the ten lepers had hope. They had heard that Jesus cured sick people and may even have touched lepers. In spite of doubts, the ten *lepers went in search of Jesus. When they found him, they got as close as they dared without causing a disturbance and asked for help.*

"Together, with humility, they pray a simple prayer. 'Jesus, master, have pity on us.' They get Jesus' attention!

"But Jesus does not immediately cure them. Instead, he gives them a bewildering command, to go and show themselves to the priests.

"This must have seemed strange to the lepers because according to Jewish law, presenting themselves to the priests was what a leper would do AFTER he was cured.

"They could have interpreted what Jesus asked as being simply wrong to do, or that he was mocking them by telling them to do something foolish and futile, and very inappropriate. But they obey. They do not protest. They pray and obey.

"There is wisdom in such actions. When you pray for something good to happen to you, it helps to behave as if you already have it! You prepare to have the gift you want. It may have been the same with the lepers.

"When they start out on their journey to the priests, their situation might have seemed doubtful, perhaps even ridiculous or hopeless. But before they had gone very far, amazing changes began to happen!

It came to pass that, as they went, they were cleansed. They were healed! Each leper must have felt new health pulsating through his veins. What was happening?

"The healing of leprosy was too good to be true. Yet it was true! They felt and saw it for themselves and in each other.

"We can imagine them standing together on the road, expressing great excitement and happiness! All had been healed! Their future could now be everything they wanted!

"Several of the lepers were likely thinking of their families, their wives and children whom they had not seen for months, perhaps years. Others may be thinking of their homes, the work they left behind or their farms. Some may have been thinking of merchandise they had once sold.

"Eagerly a few leave the group and take off to see what had happened since they left. One by one they leave in order to go home and pick up their lives. Soon, only one of the lepers is left, the Samaritan.

"The Samaritan looks down the road. There is joy on his face, perhaps mixed with bewilderment. He may have thought, 'I too have a business that I have not seen for years, and I don't know what has happened to it. I too yearn to see those I love again.'

"But something more important is pressing on his heart. He thinks of Jesus who had healed him. He does not say to himself, 'Well, as long as all the others aren't going back, I guess I don't need to return either.' Instead, he turns back, makes his way to Jesus.

"With great gratitude, the Samaritan leper kneels and expresses his deep thanks.

"Why him? Why not the others? Other than being a foreigner, what is different about this man?

"Perhaps the other nine were grateful, but did not express their gratitude. They might have said, 'Jesus knows we appreciate what he did for us.'

"We may say of those who help us, 'They know we are thankful,' But often they do not. Or maybe they reasoned, 'Jesus was just doing his job, doing what Jesus does.'

"Or possibly, the lepers became so absorbed in their gift that they forgot the giver, even the one who made their new lives possible.

"There is another possibility. The nine lepers may soon have focused their attention upon the pain and difficulties they had suffered, the unfairness, the loneliness. Perhaps their suffering left them with such bitterness they almost forgot what they had gained.

"The Samaritan who returned to give thanks had suffered as much as the other lepers, but those *dark days and nights were nearly forgotten now that he was well and filled with deep gratitude.*

"There is great sadness in Jesus' words, 'Were not ten cleansed? Where are the other nine?'

"Jesus is not expressing personal displeasure for not being appreciated, but rather concern and disappointment.

"Yes, where are the nine? Each of us needs to ask: 'Am I one of the nine; am I like them?'

"Just because the Samaritan came back does not mean he is not as excited and happy as the others were for being healed.

"No, his joy was far greater than theirs. He could not think of receiving this great healing blessing without giving thanks.

"By deciding not to give thanks, we bring about more situations in life for which we are not thankful.

"The problem with unexpressed gratitude is it doesn't lift us to experience lasting joy. When we give thanks to the giver, we are uplifted and experience grace. It is an enjoyment that constantly rekindles thankfulness for more such experiences, resulting in a life which is greatly enriched!

"At night before I go to sleep, I often do what my grandfather taught me. I review the day and ask to

recall an image of the best moment of the day. And I give thanks to God for whatever it was.

"Try it. It is enjoyable to give thanks each night for a beautiful moment. Let us fill our lives with the beauty and joy that comes from gratitude.

"For our closing prayer, we will sing the hymn of the day, which so elegantly expresses our prayer for healing during this time of COVID-19.

"We pray to heal and comfort all who are ill with the virus, for those who have suffered loss of loved ones, loss of job, loss of income. We pray to strengthen the many health professionals and others on the front lines caring for the patients.

"We will sing, "Healer of our every Ill," Hymn 612. You will find the words on the screen.

Healer of our ev'ry ill, Light of each tomorrow,
Give us peace beyond our fear,
And hope beyond our sorrow.
You who know our fears and sadness,
Grace us with your peace and gladness,
Spirit of all comfort fills our hearts.

(Text and Music by Marty Haugen)

At the end of the hymn, Pastor Maria looked directly into the camera and smiled. "Amen," she said. "Thanks be to God."

During the last verse, Ian came over to where his grandmother was seated and presented her with a picture he had drawn. It was a simple "stick" drawing of his father, mother, grandmother, and himself: Ricardo was very large, and Ian was small, Becky was larger than Ian but not as large as Ricardo or Alicia. A large round sun was shining, complete with yellow rays. Everyone, including the sun, was smiling. What was most noticeable to Alicia was what appeared to be a dog next to the child. The family did not have a dog.

"Who is that?" Alicia asked.
"That's my new dog."
"Oh, I haven't met him," said Alicia.
"I don't have him yet," said Ian.
"Oh, I see," Alicia said. "He looks like a very nice dog."
"After you go, we may get a dog," Ian said.
"Oh, that will be nice," Alicia said.

What was that all about? Alicia wondered and worried. There hadn't been any discussion about her leaving. Suddenly Alicia worried that her living with her daughter was more of an imposition than she realized. Alicia and Ian had become close. Was Becky jealous of their closeness? Alicia didn't think her daughter wanted a dog. Did Becky want her mother to leave? Was she preparing Ian?

Stop, she told herself. Why not think the best? Be thankful! Alicia had been very thankful to everyone who helped her cope when her husband died. Hospice care had been difficult. Alicia would not admit it, but more than once, she had wanted it to be OVER. But when her husband Ian finally passed, Alicia was shocked as well as heartbroken.

What would Alicia have done back in Ohio without her neighbors, her bridge-playing friends, the minister, Ian's friends -- dear people who were already drifting into past memories. Everything had changed too fast, and at the same time, very very slowly.

What would she have done without help from Ricardo, Becky and little Ian who had flown from Albuquerque to help Alicia with endings and establish a new beginning? Eventually, Becky offered her mother what Alicia had never anticipated, a home with them. "Mom, we want you to come with us--Ricardo, Ian and I. It isn't good for you to be alone. We want you to live with us."

"I'm fine," Alicia had said. "No. Absolutely not."

Nothing had happened between mother and daughter that needed forgiveness. Just annoyances. Certainly, Alicia had never expected Becky to invite her to come to Albuquerque to live with them. But after her daughter and family went home Alicia found the loneliness unbearable.

She missed her husband. Alicia missed him every morning when she awoke, every night when she went to bed alone, and in between. The house seemed to creak and groan as if to protest its near emptiness. She missed their friends and yet didn't want to see anyone. She became careless of her appearance, wearing her nightgown and robe all day.

Was she going crazy? Then Becky had called and again said, "Mom, I want you to come to Albuquerque, so I won't worry about you. I know you want your own place. That's fine. You can find a good retirement home near us, when and if you wish. But I want *you* to choose the place.

"Come and stay with us. We can visit several retirement places before you make a decision. What do you say?" Alicia had managed to hide her excitement. Yes, she wanted to go! Boy, did she want to go, but---did Becky really want her to come?

"Mom, I know we haven't always been close, but that doesn't mean we don't love each other. And you're great with Ian. You'll be a great babysitter."

"Okay," Alicia managed. "Oh, Becky, thank you. Thank you so much. I do want to come." She had even managed to say, "I love you-- and Ricardo, and Ian. Ian is ...the light of my life! Yes. Yes. I'll come."

But then COVID-19 erupted everyone's plans. In March 2020, Alicia was one of the last people who flew to Albuquerque before restrictions made it difficult if not impossible. Ian, Becky, and Recardo all met her at the airport to welcome her.

Alicia brought two large suitcases of clothing and shipped a couple of boxes of photographs and important papers. It had all happened so fast that Alicia wasn't sure what was in storage, what had been shipped, and what had been sold in the estate sale that Becky supervised.

Unfortunately, now that she was in Albuquerque, visits to retirement homes were almost non-existent, limited to virtual tours because of the serious outbreak of COVID-19 in nursing homes. They decided to give up locating a new place. Alicia had her own room. The best thing to do was simply wait for the virus to be over, wait for change. Wait for vaccines and be careful.

Becky introduced her mother to all their friends, but COVID-19 prohibited much visiting. Anyway, Alicia needed and wanted her own friends. It was going to take a while for her to feel at home. Alicia wanted to be more thankful. Pastor Maria's sermon spoke to her. Like the Samaritan she was the one who would benefit, become more fulfilled, if she had deeper gratitude. Alicia just needed to learn how.

That Sunday evening, after Ian had gone to bed and his grandmother had read him a story about a dog named

Ralph, Alicia approached her daughter. "Becky, Ian tells me he is going to get a dog when I leave."

"Oh, did he? Well, we'll see. I'm not sure about that." Becky put down her book and looked questioningly at her mother. "Oh, you don't think we--- we want you to leave do you?" With a look of exasperation, "Oh Mom. How could you think that? I was just putting it off in the future. Ian's going to miss you. I'm going to miss you! We all are! "

"I'm sorry, dear. I --I guess that makes sense. I just wondered. I am very glad to be here. I'm very grateful! But I want to find my own place when it's time. I don't want to be in the way."

When Alicia went to bed that night, she decided to believe what Becky had said, that promising Ian a dog after Alicia had left was just a practical matter. Her daughter meant well. With that thought, Alicia's heart was filled with a new deep gratitude for her daughter, for Ricardo, and especially for Ian who had included her in the picture he drew with a dog!

Alicia was so happily thankful that her body tingled, and she snuggled deeper under the covers. Before she fell asleep she asked God to bless each family member, including herself. And Alicia's heart became more loving.

As she was about to fall asleep, she gave thanks for each member of the family and then wondered, what else can I be thankful for? Reviewing her day, Alicia recalled the young woman who had checked out a few groceries for her with such enthusiasm that it had made Alicia feel blessed. Alicia gave thanks to the young woman and sent a blessing to her. And Alicia's heart became more loving.

On the third night, she recalled how Ricardo came home from work in such a good mood that he sang and waltzed his wife around their kitchen, expressing his excitement about the success he had at work.

Ricardo's exuberance brought so much joy to their home, and the more Alicia was around him, the more she laughed, and the more she admired Recardo who she once thought unworthy of her daughter.

That night Alicia gave God a big thanks for Ricardo and re-experienced the enjoyment of those moments when Ricardo sang and danced with Becky in the kitchen. And Alicia's heart became more loving.

On the fourth night, Alicia was alarmed by COVID-19 statistics in New York City, and the terrible number of deaths, the suffering of those on ventilators, the many doctors and nurses and families who were affected, the ambulance drivers and the people who were trying to help. She recalled a scene on TV where a nurse spoke tearfully of a patient dying alone without being able to see family members or say goodbye. Alicia sent healing blessings to all who had the disease and gave thanks for the protection her family received, including the masks a neighbor had made and given to them. The goodness of so many helpful people! Alicia's heart became more loving.

On the fifth night, Ian was sick with a high temperature, and they were all worried. What if he had COVID-19? They might all catch it if he did! Where might he have caught it? Children didn't often get the virus, but when they did, they could be very ill. Alicia went into Ian's bedroom. Her grandson looked up wistfully, his favorite stuffed animal, a tiger, tucked in bed beside him. Becky, who was reading a story to him paused to say, "Mom, maybe you shouldn't be in here; Ian may have the virus. If he isn't better by tomorrow, I'll call the pediatrician and have him tested; maybe we'll all be tested. Mom, you are high risk; you should stay away.'" Alicia said. "I just came in to say goodnight. Goodnight, Becky! Goodnight Ian!" She closed the door. Better not catch the virus. Before she fell asleep Alicia held the image in her mind of what she had witnessed in the bedroom--her daughter reading to her grandson. She gave thanks and sent healing blessings. And Alicia's heart became more loving.

The next morning Ian seemed fine. His high fever was gone. That evening they sent out for pizza to celebrate. Later that night, before she went to sleep, Alicia envisioned the pizza and how much the four of them enjoyed eating it. She gave thanks for the pizza, thanks for the delivery boy who brought the pizza, thanks for whoever made the pizza, for the tomatoes in the pizza sauce and whoever grew them, for the wonderful dough that made the crust, for the people who harvested the wheat to make flour to make the dough, for whoever grew the garlic for the pizza, and for those who harvested the garlic.

She gave thanks for the goblets from which they drank the wine and the grapes that made the wine, the owner of the vineyard, and the bottlers of the wine. She gave thanks for the cows that made the milk which Ian drank, and for those who milked the cows and those who bottled the milk, for the truckers who brought the milk to stores and restaurants. And also, for the pizza-cutter which cut pizza into triangular pieces, and the people who manufactured and sold the pizza cutters.

Alicia gave thanks for all of it! How fun to realize how much there was to be thankful for! Alicia's heart was more loving than it had ever been, and she was deeply thankful. She slept very, very well.

CHAPTER 6

The Parable of the Bridesmaids
Edith and Joel

<u>November 2020</u>

After devouring a hurried breakfast, an onion bagel with Havarti cheese laced with jalapeno, Edith Antonetti turned on the usual Sunday Zoom service on her computer. The virtual congregation was concluding the opening hymn. She was just a few minutes late for church.

Edith noticed that Joel Williams had joined the session without his video on, but his name appeared in the gallery indicating his presence. That Joel wasn't ready to be seen was not surprising. He probably just got out of bed and was still in his pjs. Joel would turn on the video when he was ready to be seen in Zoom's gallery images.

Edith couldn't help but be glad he was virtually present. She liked Joel, although he was more politically conservative than she and many of her friends were. Edith found Joel pleasant and fun to be with, not to mention handsome. The two had gone out a few times before COVID-19 restricted group gatherings. After their last date in April at a coffee shop, they had stopped seeing each other. Joel had looked intently at her and said, "I'm a Pete Barnum supporter," as if confessing he was a communist.

"Well, that's interesting; I'm not," she had said casually, thinking *"Damn. This romance will not be going anywhere."*

"I know," Joel responded, looking at her as if he were trying to interpret her reaction.

"I just wanted you to know."

"I sort of figured you were a Barnum supporter," Edith said, trying to sound casual.

"Maybe we can talk about politics some other time?"

"Let's not," Joel said. They shared a look that let each know they had just acknowledged their relationship was basically over. Edith and Joel's differences were as deep as the Continental Divide.

Much had changed in the last seven months due to the increased number of COVID-19 pandemic cases. Movie theaters, concerts and restaurants were no longer available to them. Both Edith and Joel had become more involved in campaign activities.

When George Floyd was killed by police in Minneapolis, Edith marched with Black Lives Matter protesters in Albuquerque. Joel made a trip to Arizona to be in a Barnum rally and didn't bother to go into quarantine when he returned, convinced that the Democrats and the media had exploited the virus, exaggerating its dangerous effects as a political motive.

Now it was the week of the presidential election. The crevice between Joel and Edith was only a small fraction of the multitude of wedges existing between millions of people throughout the country. Both sides were critical of the other side, and certain of their own perceptions. Neither side expected the election to resolve differences.

On Sunday morning Edith wondered if Pastor Maria would say anything about the 2020 presidential election scheduled for Tuesday. While she understood clergy needed to be neutral politically, Edith felt strongly that this election was about saving the country from a tragic path to dictatorship.

Joel felt very differently than Edith. Pete Barnum represented the rights of ordinary people to be free of the unnecessary government restrictions that Joel believed were hamstringing the economy. Joel believed in personal freedom and being able to own whatever guns a person wanted to have. He supported the Republican Party and did not want to succumb to unnecessary bureaucracy and an elite control of government policies based on misleading information or so-called "science. "As for the pandemic, President Barnum had been doing what he could to help the country obtain a successful vaccine. What did people expect?

When the Zoom screen focused on a smiling Pastor Maria, Joel found her a bit too happy, too bright.

"We shall sing the hymn of the day, Number 650 in your hymnal. 'In Christ there is no East or West.' A few members from our regular choir will lead the singing. Just follow the words on the screen."

> *"In Christ there is no east or west,*
> *in him no south or north,*
> *but one community of love*
> *throughout the whole wide earth."*

(Text: John Oxenham)

Really, Joel thought. *No north or south, east or west? Tell that to the Electoral College. A community of love throughout the whole wide earth?* Maybe ideally speaking, but it did not exist.

Edith was enjoying singing the hymn, even though singers on Zoom were muted. She looked forward to being in the choir when it fully started up again, and indoor services resumed.

Before the pandemic, singing together was something everyone had been able to do without regard to catching the virus. Now it was difficult to feel part of a unified group.

Pastor Maria announced the chosen parable lesson and Bible verses for the day's sermon:

"The Parable of the Bridesmaids, Matthew 25: 1-13. "Then the Kingdom of Heaven will be like ten bridesmaids who took their lamps and went to meet the bridegroom. Five of them were foolish, and five were wise. The five who were foolish didn't take enough olive oil for their lamps, but the other five were wise enough to take along extra oil. When the bridegroom was delayed, they all became drowsy and fell asleep.

"At midnight they were roused by the shout, 'Look, the bridegroom is coming! Come out and meet him!' All the bridesmaids got up and prepared their lamps. Then the five foolish ones asked the others, 'Please give us some of your oil because our lamps are going out.

"But the others replied, 'We don't have enough for all of us. Go to a shop and buy some for yourselves.'

"But while they were gone to buy oil, the bridegroom came. Those who were ready went in with him to the marriage feast, and the door was locked.

Later, when the other five bridesmaids returned, they stood outside, calling, 'Lord! Lord! Open the door for us!' But he called back, 'Believe me, I don't know you!'

"So, you, too, must keep watch! For you do not know the day or hour of my return."

"The Word of the Lord." Pastor Maria said, concluding the reading with a familiar phrase.

"Thanks be to God," Joel muttered along with the other muted Zoom viewers, including Edith.

Pastor Maria continued with her sermon:

"Weddings seem to have been as lavish in Jesus's day as they often are now, or at least were, before the pandemic. In our parable today, the ten bridesmaids (older translations refer to them as 10 virgins) had the critical role of meeting the bridegroom, welcoming him, and escorting him to the marriage feast.

"We can imagine how excited the bridesmaids were --dressed in their wedding finery, eagerly looking forward to greeting the bridegroom, escorting him to the bridal feast, and joining in on the festivities.

"But the maidens are not alike. Five of the bridesmaids are ready for the unexpected; five are not. Five of the bridesmaids wisely brought extra oil for their lamps; five foolishly had not done so.

"Often the unexpected happens at weddings; this wedding is no different. The bridegroom comes late! He does not arrive until midnight, by which time the bridesmaids have fallen asleep! Quickly, the ten maidens awaken; they trim and light their lamps, but by the time the bridegroom is ready, and the procession is moving, the lamps belonging to the foolish maidens have started going out! What can they do?

"The five foolish maidens ask the five wise maidens for some of their oil, but the wise bridesmaids say no; they tell them to go and purchase more oil for their lamps. It seems a little cruel. Couldn't they share? "No, here is a good reason for their refusal. If they did so, there might not be enough oil in the lamps to escort the Bridegroom to his destination. Doing so could result in things becoming much worse.

"What can the foolish bridesmaids do? They hurry and leave. They are able to acquire extra oil, but when they return and try to join the others on the way to the marriage feast, it is too late. They have already arrived at the feast and shut the door.

"'Lord, Lord!' they cry, "Open the Door for us." But the Lord says, "Truly, I tell you, I do not know you."

"These words, 'I do not know you,' are painful to hear. There is no excuse, no opportunity to bargain. It is painful; it is rejection.

"*The story ends with an important lesson to be learned. 'Keep watch. You do not know the day or the hour.'*

"*We do not know when the bridegroom will come or what will happen in the future. That is something we have freshly learned in this pandemic!*

"*Make the best of each day, love life, live with courage and faith-- and prepare for the unexpected!*

"*Some people think the wise bridesmaids should have shared their oil. The great American philosopher and poet, Ralph Waldo Emerson, thought they should have shared the oil they had with the other bridesmaids. Several parables teach us to share or give what we have, such as the parable of the widow's mite.*

"*But this parable states that if they had done so, all the lamps might have gone out.*

"*This does not mean we should give only from abundance. It means we are not to give away what is most essential, what defines us, what is needed to fulfill our purpose--even if others say they need it for themselves.*

"*To do so is irresponsible. Do not self-sabotage who you are and what you have been called to do. Do not violate important agreements you have made, 'to be nice.'*

"Fuel is what powers the lamps. The oil is a metaphor for the source of our power and strength. It is what empowers us. It is the divine essence in each one of us that nourishes our souls and shapes our character. It is not transferable. We can give away many things or loan them to others, but our oil, the divine power that makes us who we are, is not something we can hand over to others. In other words, do not give away your power.

"The reality in life is that we do not enter into anything that we are not somewhat prepared for. This implies we are ready--or almost so. You and I can meet whatever is coming.

"The way we prepare for tomorrow is to make the right use of today. In the future, we may need more oil. For now, we can handle what this pandemic brings--the pain, the economic problems, the illness, the suffering --even death.

"Is the foolish maidens' situation final? Is the door to the Kingdom of God permanently shut so the maidens will never enter into the Bridal Feast?

"I do not believe so.

"All of us make foolish decisions at one time or another. Hopefully, the bridesmaids will bring extra oil next time. In life, we learn to prepare. The door to the kingdom of God is open to us during our lifetimes. I tend to believe the door will not be shut permanently even in the afterlife.

"This is a special time in history. So much in life depends on our decisions, our choices. What we are today is the result of the many decisions we made in the past, some of which we may regret.

"Often we are not aware of the causes or effects of our decisions.

"At this time of COVID-19, we have more decisions than ever to make whether or not to wear masks...whether to stay home from an event or attend it. Whom to believe?

"As you all know, a presidential election is occurring this week, perhaps the most significant election in the history of our country. We are in the midst of a terrible global pandemic, and we are faced with several critical situations --unemployment, economic disasters, racial injustice, and environmental injustice.

"The decisions we make in this election will affect us for decades. Most of you have made your decisions; many have already voted, but if you have not done so already, be sure and vote! Vote for the candidates you believe will work for the greater good of our country. Respect everyone's right to do the same.

"Draw on your oil. Light your lamps accordingly. Make certain you have sufficient oil on hand to keep them lit for a long while with extra oil to lead the way to the eternal feast.

"Let us all pray."

Following the sermon, the service moved quickly through the offering, confession, forgiveness, and prayers requesting help for members of the congregation. Pastor Maria concluded with a prayer asking for wisdom and fairness in the coming election. A video of enthusiastic musicians then led the closing song, with guitars, tambourine, and drum:

This little light of mine, I'm goin' ta let it shine:
This little light of mine, I'm goin' ta let it shine:
This little light of mine, I'm goin' ta let it shine:
Let it shine, Let it shine, let it shine!
Ev-ry where I go, I'm goin' ta let it shine:
Let it shine, Let it shine, let it shine!

(Text: African American Spiritual)

Several attendees sent messages in the chat line-

"Have a great week!"
"Be well! "
"Great sermon, Pastor! "
"See you next week!"

Then, a final signal from virtual media: *The service has ended.* And a final invitation: *Leave the Meeting.* Each in their home settings, Edith and Joe closed their screens. Joel turned his computer on to a sports station to check the football schedule for the afternoon NFL game. Edith opened her Sunday newspaper.

Both reflected on how glad they were to see each other and how unfortunate it was they were not more compatible.

The two held diametrically opposing viewpoints, characteristic of many people throughout the United States. Joel was glad Pastor Maria had finally said something about the election. He had volunteered to be a poll watcher on Tuesday. Joel fervently hoped the President would be re-elected, believing Barnum had done a good job on the economy and would do even better after the pandemic subsided.

He admired the way Barnum could move through barriers and how he always was doing the unexpected. He admired Barnum's guts and lack of attention to authority. Barnum wasn't afraid of anything or anyone. He was what the country needed.

Relaxed in her apartment, Edith was reading a Sunday newspaper article about Vice President Swanson. A president should be elected on the basis of qualifications. The current president wasn't qualified for his job. At least Swanson knew what the job of president entailed because of his experience as vice president. Barnum was not a great businessman; he was a damn fine salesman, probably the best in the world, but Edith didn't think he knew much about running government.

Edith disliked how Barnum bragged all the time about making America great again or creating the best economy in the history of the country. To Edith's thinking, Barnum had inherited an economy which had been saved by the previous administration. Now due to the pandemic, the economy had the highest unemployment in decades. The stock market was doing great but that didn't help most people. Barnum was just making himself and his wealthy friends richer.

Joel didn't believe all the propaganda on the dangers of climate change. He did not think the rising ocean or warmer temperatures was caused by humanity. Yes, the climate was changing but the earth had gone through climate change cycles long before the industrial age. If the Green New Deal was enacted it would wreck the economy completely. Carbon emissions zero by 2035? Impossible! It was just a way to get votes from crazy progressive idealists.

Edith believed addressing climate change was the most important issue of the century and must be addressed before it was too late. In 10 years, the damage would be irreversible. Edith championed the Green New Deal and had been very distressed when the United States withdrew from the Paris Accord. What was wrong with people? Couldn't they see what was happening? Birds dying, hurricanes, floods, fires! The Arctic ice is melting!

Edith was even more worried about racism. The president encouraged racism! The future of the United States, if not the world, was dependent on people embracing equality. Too many people were behaving as if the United States was still fighting the civil war.

Joel believed President Barnum when he said he was not a racist. What was so terrible about seeing the positive side of some white supremacists? You'd think liberals would agree there was good in everyone!

Edith was still angry with Pete Barnum's "guy talk" in the famous video on a Hollywood bus where he bragged about how he could kiss any woman he chose. She had no respect for Barnum because he demonstrated little respect for women.

His wife, Rolanda, was beautiful and pleasant, but the relationship seemed based on Barnum's financial and social situation rather than romance. But Edith had to admit that

Rolanda didn't look miserable. Joel didn't believe any of the accusations made by porn stars about their affairs with Barnum. They were just trying to get publicity for themselves and improve their careers.

Rolanda didn't seem to mind Barnum's behavior, so why should anyone else? Several presidents had women on the side. What about John F. Kennedy, FDR, and Dwight Eisenhower? You didn't hear much about them!

Edith found Barnum's lies about COVID-19 unforgivable; he had known its dangers as early as January but continued telling people that COVID-19 was no big deal, nothing to worry about! Hundreds of thousands of people had died from it already and more would die because they believed him!

Life would never be the same for those who trusted Barnum. He rarely expressed sympathy toward people who were ill or who had lost loved ones. He didn't seem to care for anyone except himself.

Joel agreed with Barnum that only a successful vaccine would end COVID-19, and Barnum was doing everything he could to see a new vaccine be invented.

Joel thought that Barnum had done the right thing in not warning Americans about the virus earlier in the year. If Swanson were elected he would order a lockdown, and the country would never recover. Barnum understood how important it was to keep the economy going!

Joel also dislike the vice-presidential candidate, Bianca Montgomery. The reason Swanson had chosen her was because she was a black woman, and she didn't even look black. She was on the ticket only to get more votes from women, Afro-Americans and immigrants.

Joel believed Bianca Montgomery was a progressive socialist. Swanson was a moderate and he needed progressive votes. Why was there so much fuss about electing a first woman? It wasn't like women were another species.

Edith was surprised at how emotional she felt about Bianca Montgomery becoming vice president. Women had been slighted for way too long. It was 100 years since women had the right to vote, way past time for a woman to be elected president or vice president.

Edith felt Swanson and Montgomery genuinely cared for people and related to their problems. They would work for the common good. Barnum cared only for one person--himself.

According to Joel, electing Swanson and Montgomery would be going backward. Barnum ignored bureaucrats and moved forward on his own. He was not part of the deep state and didn't worry if he upset the old ways of doing things.

As for vice-presidential candidates, McGee did whatever Barnum said. Montgomery had lots of ideas and insisted on being heard! Joel agreed with McGee about abortion, but wasn't sure it should be illegal; it was a personal issue. He was impressed by McGee's calm ways. He was unflappable.

Edith disliked Vice President McGee. Yes, he was a nice man, but he didn't understand that women need control over their own bodies. He had no sympathy for what many pregnant women face. If the courts rejected Roe vs Wade, thousands of women's lives would be affected. Many would die.

And so, their contrasting thoughts ---went. Edith thought about phoning Joel, but she decided not to. Joel thought about phoning Edith, but he decided not to. Both thought of each other and both worried about the results of the election. Each day brought bad news; each day brought new hope.

On Tuesday, election night, the Democrats lost Florida! Edith was worried. She didn't go to bed until midnight, and she did not sleep well!

Joel cheered on Tuesday when it was announced that Barnum won Florida! A good omen! The Presidential race was still too close to call when Joel fell asleep in his chair.

- Wednesday morning headline, *Albuquerque Journal*: 11/4/2020: *To the wire! Vote counting continued in several key battleground states.*

- Thursday morning headline: 11/5/2020: *Swanson edges closer to White House. Michigan and Wisconsin called for Democrats.* Inside: *Barnum supporters demand 'Stop the count!'*

- Friday morning headline: 11/6/2020 *Virus Deaths, Hospitalizations up.* (COVID-19 had moved the election off the center of the page.) Sidebar: *Barnum questions election integrity, Unsupported accusations come from White House.*

- Saturday morning headline: 11/7/2020: *Swanson standing at the Edge, "We're going to win."* Inside: Pro-Barnum crowds decry count.

- Sunday morning headline: November 8, 2020: *"The time to heal," Swanson says; Barnum refuses to concede.* Inside: *Elation and anger: Catharsis in the streets as the election ends.*

Edith cried tears of happiness when Bianca Montgomery spoke from the stage: "While I might be the first woman in this office, I will not be the last..."

Many people on the streets were celebrating. A jubilant spirit was palpable. Horns were honking. Some people wore white while others waved flags. Many sang songs! For the Swanson supporters, it was as if a war had ended. But it was not a universal spirit.

Joel drove to Santa Fe for a "Truth Rally" at the state capital and watched speakers charge election fraud, wave flags and shout, "Four more years!", "Stop the Steal," "Live Free or Die."

There was no evidence of voter fraud, but clearly Barnum and supporters were going to take their case to court. Joel wished Barnum had won, and believed Barnum would have come into his own and done great things in his second term. He feared Swanson was going to be nothing but a same-old-same-old politician.

But while Joel was a solid Barnum supporter, he believed Barnum had lost the election. From what he perceived, in spite of all the fuss he heard about the election, the officials, workers, and poll watchers had been cautious.

Edith took to heart what Swanson said about recovering the soul of America. Like the fuel for the foolish bridesmaids' lamps, a nation's soul was the source of its power.

Soul was the very essence of what makes a person or a country who or what it was meant to be. Soul was about truth.

Joel was surprised Sunday night when Edith called. Why would she be calling? Was she trying to rub it in that Barnum had lost? He would not do that to her if Swanson had lost.

Nevertheless, he picked up the phone.

"Hello," he said, a bit testily.

"Hi," Edith said. "I've been thinking about you."

"That's nice," he said.

"I-- I just wanted to talk to you again," Edith said. "We disagree about a lot, but I understand how you must feel. I know how I would feel if Swanson had lost."

"Well, it may not be over," Joel pointed out.

"Of course, I am glad Swanson won. Very glad, but I miss talking to you, miss seeing you. Joel, Swanson got the most votes, but I realize 70 million people voted for Barnum. He can't be all bad."

"That's kind of--kind of you to say," Joel said.

"I mean it."

"Well, I support Swanson on one thing. It's time to heal," Joel said.

"Does that mean...?"

A moment of thick silence.

"When can I come over?" he asked.

"How about right now?"

"Be right there!" Joel promised.

Edith rejoiced, but realized it was probably a temporary truce. Like the bridesmaids in the parable, each had their own oil, which included ingredients loyal to their specific power sources. Edith and Joel's feelings about the presidential candidates were sincere and deep. Their beliefs were equally solid, reflecting the values of their souls. This would likely change for each or both of them, depending on what happened in the future, and how they responded to unknown outcomes. While Joel and Edith wished to become closer and were very attracted to one another, both sensed they needed life partners more similar to their own paths.

CHAPTER 7
The Prodigal Son
Robert II, Robbie III and Beth

Robbie would graduate from Sandia Preparatory School in just a few weeks. He was not looking forward to it. All classes had been virtual until February when students were given the choice of virtual or in-person learning. What a relief it had been to have in-class learning, but all too short. Now, after only a few months, his senior year will be over! Soon they would all graduate and go their separate ways.

The most difficult thing for Robbie was that he wasn't playing in a band anymore. Throughout high school, he had played his alto sax both in the Rio Rancho Community Band and also the jazz band at Sandia prep, neither of which were now active. Robbie also had been playing with a band comprised of his friends from high school, the Desert Sand Dusters. During his freshman and sophomore years, he had hoped to eventually major in music-- with a minor in performance-- but his parents expected him to be headed for law school and his father's law firm.

Robert Ackerman II, his father, was a senior partner in an independent law office specializing in Elder Law--estate planning, trusts, wills and bequests. Robbie had spent the last three summers working at Ackerman, Pierce and Associates and occasionally helped out during the year working on several special projects. It was a place that offered opportunity, and Robbie was expected to spend his future pursuing that opportunity.

Robbie got along well with the staff, some of whom had known him since he was a small child. His father's cranky but beloved assistant, Marilyn, kept Robbie informed about what was going on in the entire office--whom to trust, listen to, obey or ignore. She was always right.

Robbie didn't feel excited about becoming a lawyer, but it seemed like the natural thing to do. Robbie didn't dislike his family's plans for him enough to rebel. Robbie had a couple of friends who had rebelled; one had even run away for several months. Robbie wasn't going to make any waves, at least not until after he graduated

Sunday morning and Robbie was warmly greeted by his mother, Beth, as he slipped into the family room, just before the morning sermon started over Zoom. Obviously pleased to have her son join her, Beth greeted her only child with a warm smile.

Robert Ackerman II was out on the golf course, his usual Sunday morning activity, and mother and son didn't mind. Robbie Ackerman III sat down on the wide sofa beside Beth, who reached over and kissed him on his cheek just as the service began. Pastor Maria was ready to read the lesson of the day.

"The Parable of the Prodigal Son," Pastor Maria began.

"Jesus said, "There was a man who had two sons. The younger of them said to his father, 'Father, give me the shares of the property that will belong to me.' So, he divided his property between them. A few days later the younger son gathered all he had and traveled to a distant country, and there he squandered his property in dissolute living.

"When he had spent everything, a severe famine took place throughout that country, and he began to be in need. So, he went and hired himself out to one of the citizens of that country, who sent him to his fields to feed the pigs. He would gladly have filled himself with the pods that the pigs were eating, and no one gave him anything.

"But when he came to himself he said, 'How many of my father's hired hands have bread enough to spare, but here I am dying of hunger! I will get up and go to my father, and I will say to him, 'Father, I have sinned against heaven and before you; I am no longer worthy to be called your son; treat me like one of your hired hands.' So he set off and went to his father. But while he was still far off, his father saw him and was filled with compassion; he ran and put his arms around him and kissed him.

"Then the son said to him, 'Father, I have sinned against heaven and before you; I am no longer worthy to be called your son.' But the father said to his slaves, 'Quickly, bring out a robe—the best one—and put it on him; put a ring on his finger and sandals on his feet. And get the fatted calf and kill it and let us eat and celebrate; for this son of mine was dead and is alive again; he was lost and is found!' And they began to celebrate.

"Now his elder son was in the field; and when he came and approached the house, he heard music and dancing. He called one of the slaves and asked what was going on. He replied, 'Your brother has come, and

your father has killed the fatted calf, because he has got him back safe and sound.' Then he became angry and refused to go in. His father came out and began to plead with him. But he answered his father, 'Listen! For all these years I have been working like a slave for you, and I have never disobeyed your command, yet you have never given me even a young goat so that I might celebrate with my friends. But when this son of yours came back, who has devoured your property with prostitutes, you killed the fatted calf for him!'

"Then the father said to him, 'Son, you are always with me, and all that is mine is yours. But we had to celebrate and rejoice because this brother of yours was dead and has come to life; he was lost and has been found.

"The story of the prodigal son is one of the most popular parables in the Bible. It is a story with special significance today as we begin to lift the veil of the pandemic and return to what we hope is a "new normalcy."

"Whenever we hear a story, we usually identify with some of the characters. In this story we have a father, the prodigal son and an older brother. You may identify most closely with one of the three, but you may also find something to learn from each character.

"The word prodigal means reckless or lavish. The prodigal son asks for his inheritance ahead of schedule so he can have a good time; we might call it a wild time. Eventually, he ends up in trouble, reduced to

taking care of swine in a culture where pork is considered unclean.

"Because he is so poor he does not have enough to eat. The prodigal son has hit bottom!

"As you are aware, some people have hit bottom during the pandemic. Many came very close to it. Even if you have not endured great hardships you likely have friends or family who suffered greatly, died or became seriously ill. Over a half million people in the United States have now died. And it isn't over yet!

"In some ways, we have all been away in the far country, even if we have rarely left our homes throughout the pandemic. While our adventures may not be as dramatic as squandering our fortunes, we may have felt lost, and we may have realized what is most important to us.

"As we begin our exodus from many of the pandemic's restrictions, just like the prodigal son, we may have examined and rediscovered our true selves.

"Like the prodigal son, we have changed.

"I believe most are returning with a deeper spirituality and a keener sense of our dependency on others.

"We hope to create a new normalcy, one which is kinder and more considerate of others, especially to

our caretakers who have been so important to helping us.

"I believe we are now more in touch with the essential divinity found in every person, even when it is covered up, undernourished, or wounded. Whether small and nearly inaccessible or richly and gracefully developed, the spirit of the divine exists in each and every human being.

"When the prodigal son comes to himself he has a realization: the person I am being is not the true me. I am more than this! I will go home and work for my father in whatever capacity is available. I am still his son. I do not need to lead such a miserable life.

"The prodigal son did not expect a warm welcome when he arrived home, but he was confident his father would provide him with a basic job. He would not want his son to starve.

"But to his amazement, his father is thrilled to see him. He runs to meet him and presents him with a beautiful new robe, fresh sandals and a ring on his finger!

"The father then calls for a celebration with music and dancing. The son who was lost is found! The prodigal son has returned home.

"Yes, he has returned. But what will happen after the excitement is gone. Has the prodigal son really changed?

"We don't know for certain if he goes back to his old ways. Even if he does slip, fall and leave home again, his return is to be celebrated!

"Many of us returning from the far country of the pandemic also wonder: will we return to our old ways?

"Have we learned something valuable from handling the COVID-19 ordeal, to change how we want to live and maintain it in the future?

"In the coming months, we will be planning our church's future ministry. Just as the prodigal son came to himself, this is our time to come to ourselves as a congregation.

"The world has changed during this pandemic. We need to see what changes we need to make and what needs to be preserved.

"What about the older son? The older son is not celebrating his younger brother's return. He does not like all the attention his brother is getting. It is while working in the fields that the older son learns of his younger brother's arrival by hearing the music and dancing! The father had never given the older son a party like that or killed the fatted calf for him.

"Life is unfair when it comes to reward systems. Rewards are not a worthy goal; at the best, rewards are a happy, unanticipated result.

"Enjoy rewards when they come, but do not expect or gauge your worth on rewards! Doing so can send you in the wrong direction!

"The prodigal son did not come home expecting a party. The older brother gauges success in life too much on materialistic and social rewards.

"Life is essentially about finding out who we are, determining our major life purpose, living each day the best we can, and being part of God's kingdom.

"Perhaps the older brother should have gone to the far country! He seems to be caught up by too many feelings of obligation which has led to resentment.

"When he complains, his father asks the older son to realize the blessings they have enjoyed together over the years, and the legacy awaiting him.

"The older brother needs to come to himself. In recognizing the blessings of his life, by experiencing gratitude, he would become able to perceive the divinity in his younger brother, his father, himself, the servants, and all human beings.

"Will the older brother change? Again, we don't know, because it is beyond the story, but I like to think he probably does. I hope he realizes the deeper relationship he can have with his younger brother.

"It is his choice whether to accept, love and enjoy his younger brother and even learn something from him, or continue to be resentful and jealous.

"Lastly, let us also consider the father. While this is a parable about the heavenly father, the story teaches us valuable lessons about parenthood, and our roles as models for the next generation.

"One message might be to realize that it is sometimes necessary to escape to a "far country." If your child or children go, and hopefully return, warmly welcome them back.

"We need to teach our children to be responsible for their choices, and to be truthful to themselves about who they are. We must strive to do our best for our children without our egos getting in the way or overly protecting them.

"Most importantly, the great significance of "The Prodigal Son" is that the story not only reveals God's love and compassion to humanity but also reveals the divinity in humanity.

"God forgives us and invites us to come home.

"We are coming home! This is a historical time for us. Soon we will once again gather together in person and for the first time in a long time we will have services in our sanctuary.

"Our physical return to church services will be on Pentecost Sunday, the day we celebrate, when the Holy Spirit came to the place where the disciples had gathered following Jesus' crucifixion.

"Like the prodigal son, we are coming home and like his father and his brother, who hopefully continued to grow in love and understanding, we celebrate the prodigal son's return-- and our return.

"For our sermon hymn we shall sing Hymn 781, led again by choir members on zoom:" The choir and members on zoom then sang the following:

> *Children of the Heavenly Father*
> *Safely in his bosom gather:*
> *Nestling bird nor star in heaven*
> *Such a refuge e'er was given.*
>
> *Though he giveth or he taketh,*
> *God his children ne'er forsaketh;*
> *His the loving purpose solely*
> *To preserve them pure and holy.*

(Carolina Sandell Berg, tr. Ernest W. Olson. Swedish Folk Tune)

"Let us all pray...." Robbie bowed his head, as he sat next to his mother in their home. But after the prayer, Robbie stood up and stretched.

"Did you like the sermon?" his mother asked.

"Yes, yes I did. It gave me a lot to think about."

"Want to say more? Would you like some breakfast?"

"I'd love it!" Robbie answered.

"I'm just confused, Mom. I've been thinking. I'm not so sure... not sure I want to go to the University of Texas."

"Really? I thought you were happy about going there! You better talk to your Dad. And soon."

They headed for the kitchen. Robbie found the parable about the prodigal son almost too interesting. He knew several brothers who did not get along well with each other. Nothing new about that! But having the guts to come home when you have screwed up everything like that guy was not something Robbie would want to do.

Robbie had planned to begin pre-law studies at the University of Texas in the fall. The University of Texas was his father's Alma Mater, and it had a high national rating. Robbie would have preferred to study law at the University of New Mexico, while not one of the top law schools in the country, had a lot going for it, including an excellent reputation for Environmental Law.

Robbie wasn't prodigal. He was not reckless or "spendy," but he would like at some point to be more on his own, make his own way. Robbie Ackerman III needed to come to himself, to know if he wanted the life that his father was preparing for him.

Whatever choice he made, there would be regrets. He liked his father's law firm and the lifestyle the law firm afforded their family. He didn't want to rebel. But somehow he had to make his life his own. He would talk with his Dad that night.

On that evening, after his father turned off the news, they had a chance to talk:

Robbie: Dad, I've been thinking. I'm not so sure I want to go to the University of Texas. I like going into law. I really do, I think I can be a good lawyer. But I need to have my music too. I'd like to stay here in Albuquerque, take pre-law at UNM. They have a good department.

Robert: What? The University of Texas has one of the top law schools in the country! No, Son, you want the best for yourself! I'm proud of you. You've been accepted there! Your acceptance has even been published on Sandia's Matriculation Class List.

Robbie: Well, that list doesn't make it final. That's just to show where everyone's heading. Anyway, soon I'll graduate-- it will all be history.

Robert: I think you're just nervous. You'll do fine. You'll see. Once you get to Austin, you'll see what a great place it is.

Robbie: I don't think I want to go there. UNM has a good law school, Dad. They have an excellent reputation for Environmental law.

Robert: Environmental Law! When did you get interested in Environmental Law! It's got attention now, but I don't think it will last. It's way...way too political.

Robbie: I'm sort of interested. But--

Robert: But what? What? Son, don't you realize the opportunity you have? Don't throw it away!

Robbie: I'm not throwing anything away, Dad. I really liked working at your office. I liked everyone there. But...

Robert: Look, this isn't just about you coming into my office! This is about taking advantage of a great opportunity at the University of Texas! We visited there. You liked it. What is this about for God's sake? Is this about a girl?

Robbie: No, it is not about Nancy, It's more about---

Robert: About what?

Robbie: Well, my music. My sax.

Robert: Your sax? I'm sure they have music in Texas. You've heard about the Austin City Limits Music Festival?

Robbie: Yes, sure, but-

Robert: But what?? Is it this Environmental Law idea that has gotten you confused?

Robbie: I'm sorry, Dad. I'm just not sure I want to do estate planning all my life. I know it's important but ...

Robert: But what for God's sake?

Robbie: The environment-- the environment is important to... We don't have much time to make changes. I--I

Robert: Robbie, I've never asked you to do anything that you truly don't feel right about. I'm sure as hell not going to insist you go to a school where you don't want to go, even though we're talking about a hell of a fine school. You're 18 years old now! You're just scared of the future. When you get there, you'll know what's important to you.

Robbie: But--

Robert: But WHAT?

Robbie: What if it is the wrong choice? It--it doesn't feel like it's my choice. What you do in your office is important, but

Robert: But what?

Robbie: Well, I like--. I'd like to go into Environmental law-- It it is so important! There is nothing more important! It's our future!

Robie: Listen, son, you have two choices throughout life. You either make the right choice, or you make your choice right! Works every time!

Robbie: I don't want to argue.

Robert: Don't you realize this is a fantastic opportunity for you-- to become part of my office. I can't believe it! What's the matter with you?

Robbie: I don't know. I really don't. I appreciate everything you do, Dad, I really do, but.

Robert: But what? What?

Robbie could hardly speak: This is my life and...

Robert: AND WHAT? Why didn't we have this talk before? Don't you realize what you have and what you are giving up. C'mon now, Champ! I'd like you to go to the University of Texas where I went! We'll talk about this later.

Robbie looked down. There was nothing more he could say. He needed his father's blessing.

Robert: C'mon. You'll be coming home every once in a while. You won't lose your connections here.

Robbie: I don't want to go there, Dad. I am sorry, but I don't.

Robert: Okay. I'll tell you what. Take pre-law at the University of Texas next year. I think you will like it-- maybe love it, like I did. But if you still want to change after a year. I will.... I may not like it, but I'll honor your decision if you want to go into Environmental Law wherever you want to go, even though I don't think is a good idea. I promise.

Robbie couldn't believe his ears. He nodded and smiled. It would give them a year, and it would be worth it to not upset his dad now. This would give them both time to adjust. Robbie would still be loyal to himself.

Robert: Pray about it. Ask for guidance. But be clear. Take one step at a time.

Robbie couldn't help but think about the prodigal son. The University could be a good place to spend a year. It wasn't exactly a far country to think things through, but it gave him and his father some time. Neither would likely change their minds, but his Dad would not forget their agreement. Robbie was thankful.

CHAPTER 8

The Laborers in the Vineyard

Kaitlin and Neil,
Rebecca, Gertrude, Samuel Goldstein

SNOWBRAINS HEADLINE: 2020-2021, *"FACTALITIES"*; DEATHS; STATE AVERAGE DOUBLES

The last ten winters, an average of 27 people died in avalanches each winter season in the United States. This season alone, the United States has reported 36 avalanche fatalities. This winter, the state of Colorado alone has experienced twelve of these fatalities, more than double the state's average over the last five seasons. This statistic marks the highest amount of avalanche deaths in the centennial state since the winter of 1992-1993 and tied for the most Colorado has seen in over a century.

(2020-2021 Colorado Avalanche Deaths Most Since Winter of 1992-1993. Ryan Flynn, April 21, 2021, snowbrains.com)

Months had now passed since Kaitlin Adams received the call that changed her life forever. It was from her boyfriend Neil's young sister,

Rebecca: "Kaitlin, there has been a terrible accident near Mineral Creek. An avalanche."

"What? What happened? Is Neil all right?" Kaitlin asked, expecting her to answer, "Oh yes, he's fine." But that was not her response.

"No. He's not all right," Rebecca answered in a surprisingly calm voice. "He's dead, Kaitlin. He is buried in 20 feet of snow."

"What? I don't understand! Not Neil. He was always so careful!"

"He is...gone," Rebecca interrupted. "There were three casualties, and Neil was one of them. They'll be excavating again tomorrow because there is so much debris from the avalanche. They need a helicopter in order to recover the bodies, but that won't be until tomorrow-- or as soon as they can."

Kaitlin could not possibly believe Neil-- *had died! Died?* Everyone, including Kaitlin, expected them to marry someday.

"No. Please God, No. Not Neil. I can't believe it. I won't believe it!... I should have been with him."

"Mom and Dad asked me to call you. The Rabbi is with them now. My mother and father can't talk right now. They know how much you and Neil cared for each other. Mom said to ask you if you wanted to come here, come to our house. Mom doesn't want you to be alone. Do you want to come over here?"

Kaitlin did not want to be alone, but she had been with the Goldsteins for dinner only a few times and always with Neil. Always! She and Neil weren't even engaged, although they had been a couple for more than five years and were both in their 30s. They should have gotten married before it was too late!

"We're having shivah tomorrow night at 7:00," Rebecca said. "Please come. Neil would want you to be here."

"I understand. Yes, I'll come tomorrow. I'll be okay."

Reality was beginning to set in. Kaitlin could hardly breathe.

"I should have been with him! I wish I had been with him. I-- I can't imagine life without him." Kaitlin heard herself weep in sobs she didn't at first recognize as her own.

"I know," said Rebecca, sharing her own feelings, almost losing control.

Kaitlin was stunned. Could it be possible that she would never ever see Neil again? That they would never laugh again together, sleep together again? Go to ball games, ski, dance, and someday-- marry? Could her future, their future, totally disappear?

Then she remembered their friend Jacob.

"What about Jacob?" Kaitlin asked. Jacob had gone with Neil on the ski trip.

"He survived. Jacob is in the hospital. He deployed his airbag and was dug out but lost his skis and poles."

Rebecca was also weeping now; she had handled about as much as she possibly could but managed to continue. "May I ask you to call other friends in your group? Molly and Sam, Jean, Ezra, Henry, Deborah, and others you may know. Maybe one of them can call the others and let them know what happened. I need to call some relatives."

"Yes, Yes, of course." Kaitlin agreed. If she called her friends, someone would come to comfort her; she would not be alone. Her entire future now meant being alone, maybe forever, never with Neil.

Somehow Kaitlin thanked Rebecca for calling and their painful phone call ended. Why had she not gone with him?

For a few seconds, Kaitlin recalled how she and Neil first met on the ski hill in Santa Fe. Skiing was Neil's life.

Kaitlin wasn't as good a skier as Neil. Neil had invited her to accompany him on this last trip, but Kaitlin was not as confident as Neil when it came to skiing in the backcountry. She didn't want to hold him back.

But if she had gone with him, this accident probably would not have happened. What on earth had happened?

In the next four months of grief, loneliness, and constant regret, Kaitlin became familiar with numerous reports and statistics about the accident. She wanted to know what had happened, but it didn't help much to find out.

Neil was the third of the four young men who were skiing down the mountain when the avalanche released, catching all four riders. Jacob, who survived, was the last one down. His three friends were buried under debris that was extremely deep, up to 20 feet, and very heavy.

In the recovery operation, helicopters dropped explosives to protect searchers. They used power tools to recover the bodies. The three skiers who were killed were found about 100 yards from each other, buried nine, eleven, and twenty feet deep.

In the next few months, Kaitlin became accustomed to having nightmares. In each nightmare, she was snowshoeing in the mountains. Snow was coming down extremely hard, making headway nearly impossible. She was looking for Neil... searching for Neil, unable to find him in the dense snowstorm.

Kaitlin became closer to Neil's mother, Gertrude Goldstein, but not his father, Samuel. The loss of his older son, Neil, had left a huge hole in his heart, and he responded by isolating himself with grief.

Kaitlin also became good friends with Rebecca, and with Neil's younger brother Adam, a freshman in high school. But gradually Kaitlin saw less of the Goldstein family. She no longer had a role that didn't stir tragic feelings.

Neil and Kaitlin had talked about marriage, but there had been no engagement. The differences in their religions had been a factor in their constant postponements, but they had agreed it was not going to be the determiner. They respected each other's religion and did not want to abandon their respective faiths. They treasured and honored each other's independence.

Now, there seemed to be nothing to hold Kaitlin to her boyfriend's family, and while they would always share fond memories, she needed to find new paths.

What bothered Kaitlin the most was the why question - *Why?* All of the skiers were experienced and cautious. They loved the isolated beauty, the adventure, and the powdery snow of the backcountry.

What kind of universe and what kind of God allowed such things as avalanches and COVID-19 to kill good people? That was the question on Kaitlin's mind the Sunday morning she was watching Pastor Maria on Zoom.

The depth of Kaitlin's grief and increasing depression was not well known at the church. Neil had accompanied her to occasional services, such as holidays and concerts. Most people knew Kaitlin's Neil had passed away and felt sad for her and curious about the avalanche, but they hadn't known Neil well, and they didn't know Kaitlin very well either. She kept a distance from everyone.

Sometimes Kaitlin found herself wishing Neil's death had been caused by COVID-19. If Neil had died from the virus the two would have been part of a larger tragedy. There would be more understanding, and she would have had more company and shared more grief. The couple had been very careful to wear masks and to obey the governor's mandates. Kaitlin was now vaccinated; Neil would have been vaccinated if he were still alive. Her thoughts were ridiculous, and she knew it, but her feelings were real.

The real issue for Kaitlin was to get over her anger, her questioning of God, the reasonableness of life itself, and find a way to go on. How could she pray or be a part of the church when she felt so betrayed by the pain and death God allowed people to experience—COVID-19, avalanches or whatever?

Kaitlin could not help but be disappointed in God! Couldn't he have included built-in safety nets, especially for good people like Neil?

Before the Zoom service began, before she turned on her computer, Kaitlin took time to pray: "Please God, help me understand. Help me accept your ways."

Pastor Maria announced the opening hymn, ironically, Number 771, "*God the Sculptor of the Mountains*" led by members of the choir. The hymn was unknown to Kaitlin but interesting; the melody was familiar.

> *God the sculptor of the mountains*
> *God the miller of the sand*
> *God the jeweler of the heavens*
> *God the potter of the land:*
> *You are the womb of all creation,*
> *We are formless; shape us now.*

(text: John Thornburg)

It was time for the sermon. Pastor Maria stepped forward to the lectern and cleared her throat: *"Today's*

sermon will be on the Parable of the Landowner, Matthew 20
1-16.

"For the kingdom of heaven is like a landowner
who went out early in the morning to hire workers for
his vineyard. He agreed to pay them a denarius for the
day and sent them into his vineyard.

"About nine in the morning he went out and
saw others standing in the marketplace doing nothing.
He told them, 'You also go and work in my vineyard,
and I will pay you whatever is right.' So, they went. He
went out again about noon and about three in the
afternoon and did the same thing. At about five in the
afternoon, he went out and found still others standing
around. He asked them, 'Why have you been standing
here all day long doing nothing?' 'Because no one has
hired us,' they answered. He said to them, 'You also go
and work in my vineyard.'

"When evening came, the owner of the
vineyard said to his foreman, 'Call the workers and pay
them their wages, beginning with the last ones hired
and going on to the first.' The workers who were hired
about five in the afternoon came and each received a
denarius.

"When those who came and were hired first,
they expected to receive more. But each one of them
also received a denarius. When they received it, they
began to grumble against the landowner. 'These who
were hired last worked only one hour,' they said, 'and

you have made them equal to us who have borne the burden of the work and the heat of the day.'

"But he answered one of them, 'I am not being unfair to you, friend. Didn't you agree to work for a denarius? Take your pay and go. I want to give the one who was hired last the same as I gave you. Don't I have the right to do what I want with my own money? Or are you envious because I am generous?'

"So the last will be first, and the first will be last.

"The word of the Lord. Pastor Maria stated.

"Thanks be to God."

Pastor Maria continued with her sermon.

"The Laborers in the Vineyard" is either one of the easiest or one of the most difficult parables to interpret. The story is straightforward, but we find its message puzzling. We can't help but judge the owner in the parable to be unfair. Is God unfair?

"From a materialistic or commercial perspective, the answer has to be yes. When it comes to rewards, the Kingdom of God is very different from the commercial and material world we live in.

"We live in both worlds--the Kingdom of God and the commercial, material world. We need to realize the differences, not confuse them and not apply one set of values to where it is non-existent.

"In the parable, we are told the workers are paid one denarius for their labor, or about 20 cents a day. Today, there is an effort to have basic wages set at $15.00 an hour. Quite a difference in scale, but it doesn't change the meaning.

"The vineyard is a familiar setting for us; we can easily identify with the many vineyards here in Albuquerque. In New Mexico, we have chili pickers. This year at the Rosales farm in Lemitar, NM, due to a labor shortage, only five men, Mexican nationals, harvested chilies in the Rosales chile fields. They worked from 6:30 AM to 4:30 pm; and were paid on the basis of how many sacks they picked rather than their time in the field. At the Rosales farm, they are paid $3.00 for every 50-pound sack of chiles, and they pick 40 to 50 sacks a day, which is a great deal of money for a person who doesn't have work.

"In spite of the hard work and their expenses, Mexican workers are able to send considerable money home to care for their families.

"Because the wages are based on productivity (the number of sacks gathered), there is no controversy about payment based on the amount of time spent in the fields.

"According to the Albuquerque Journal, Linda Rosales wishes the United States would make it easier for Mexican nationals to work in the fields because it

has become much more difficult for them to cross the border.

"According to Linda, hiring American workers for harvesting chile has not been successful even during low employment, because Americans are unaccustomed to hard labor in the scorching heat."

(Albuquerque Journal, October 3, 2020, page A16)

"What if the Mexican farm workers were each paid $30 for their work, no matter whether they picked 10 sacks or 50 sacks? Surely, they would protest if they had picked 50 sacks and worked all day, and a fellow worker received the same amount of money for picking 10 sacks of chiles. They probably would not continue picking 50 sacks a day and only pick only a few.

"What will become of us without our favorite chiles?"

"This parable is about the Kingdom of God, which has a totally different arrangement than business or industry when it comes to rewarding human behavior.

"We have a very hard time accepting it because we evaluate human worth in materialistic and commercial terms.

"But the parable is very clear. Things are valued differently in God's kingdom, and we need to realize it.

"We keep trying to live our lives as if we are machines and the kingdom of God is based on a reward system similar to laboring in a factory or field.

"In the parable, the owner tells the foreman to pay the workers who come last first, the same amount as the workers who came first and worked all day. All are paid the same!

"Those who come early complained loudly, because they felt taken advantage of, even though they agreed to the terms. We understand their feelings!

"The owner says, "I have done you no wrong. I paid you what was agreed upon. Why are you jealous because I am generous?

"But income inequality is a great problem today. Labor unions have lost a lot of their power. Today we have a vast number of people who must work more than one job.

"It was recently reported in the news that a pharmaceutical executive was receiving $121 million a year in salary compared to workers on the frontline who were susceptible to COVID-19 hazards and who are working for less than $15.00 an hour!

"Something is morally wrong with such inequity!

"Clearly, Jesus is not recommending a policy for industry or business, or not-for-profit

organizations. He is telling us about the kingdom of God and how different it is from commercial reality.

"The Kingdom of God does not operate on a reward system; life is not about acquiring material rewards; it is beyond commercial values. It is not the motive; it is the goal, and the rewards are not materialistic.

"In the Kingdom of God, people do what is good and right for its own sake. What is rewarding commercially, materially speaking, is not grounds for rewards in God's kingdom.

"Our creator God 'maketh his sun rise on the evil and on the good. And sends rain on the just and on the unjust (Matthew 5, v.45)'

"This parable is simply a statement of fact. The creation, nature, is impartial. It does not discriminate. Nature acts without regard to moral character. The sun shines, the rain falls on the fields without regard to the moral and religious differences of owners.

"The chiles yield just as much for the most stingy farmers as they do in the fields of the most generous. If we regard nature and the universe as purely objective, we have no difficulty. The interflow of forces and influences in productivity whether for good or evil may seem unfair, but each of us experiences proof of the indifference of nature.

"Nature does not distinguish between virtue and vice, even though it is affected. Fires burn homes belonging to good people as well as homes which belong to criminals. The sun rises and sets. Clouds gather and sweep by. Tides ebb and flow. Grass grows. Apples ripen and fall.

"We are all equally vulnerable to nature's violence and to nature's kindness. This does not mean God is indifferent. In nature, we see the open hand of our Mother and Father God. Nature treats all of us the same.

"In every ray of sunshine that falls from heaven. In every drop of rain that waters the fruitful ground, I hear the words, 'This is God's impartial kindness to all of you. We are all his children.'

"We strive to treat our own children equally. We do not expect every child to be the same but as teachers and parents, it is up to us to provide each child with love and care, no strings attached.

"Rewards in the Kingdom of God are not materialistic, hypocritical, for notoriety, nor given to improve productivity or match human timetables. And there are spiritual rewards! We enjoy many wonderful spiritual rewards: peace, bliss, joy, grace, love, eternal life. Materialistic rewards pale in comparison.

"Each of us is invited to the Kingdom of God. Some respond and come early while others receive and

respond late in life. All receive the same spiritual rewards.

"Thanks be to God. Amen."

As Pastor Maria ended the sermon, Kaitlin recalled something Neil would often say that she had found puzzling, "When you go against reality, you lose 100% of the time." Neil once said that almost everyone chooses to go up against reality at one time or another. Does one always know what is reality, and what is truth?

During the past months, Kaitlin had studied the Colorado Avalanche Information Center report, over and over. The painful truth was that Neil had gone up against reality and he had lost. It had cost him his life. Being expert skiers, the four men had let themselves believe they were immune from disaster.

The foursome was skiing through avalanche terrain and while they moved carefully, one skier at a time, it was the warmest day so far that year, 32 degrees for several hours. They were over 12 thousand feet elevation, and the slope angle was 40 degrees.

Kaitlin was no expert, but she knew the conditions were dangerous.

Likely, Neil had also realized it was dangerous, but perhaps he had reasoned it would be safe enough. Nothing had saved him. Nothing. Not God. Not Kaitlin. Not himself.

He had gone with the group decision. Three of them died. One lived. Nature is non-discriminatory.

Neil and Kaitlin would never have a future together. She wanted to be able to forgive him for that.

Kaitlin vowed to always remember and treasure Neil as her beloved, a wonderful man with whom she had known persistent happiness, someone she would always love, this man Neil who loved her so dearly and died so young.

His memory, his presence, would continue to be important in her life.

Neil was not long in the vineyard, but he had meant so much to her; he always would. She hoped they would meet again.

CHAPTER 9

The Hidden Treasure and
The Pearl of Great Price
(Kurt, Bo, Clyde, Clare, Hank, Joellen, Ava and Andy)

PROLOGUE: (10 Months Earlier):

Kurt Gordon was one of New Mexico's first COVID-19 casualties. He died on May 9, 2020, when the virus was still new, and its danger was not fully grasped. He was 65 years old.

Clyde, the head nurse in the ICU, had called Kurt's son, Bo, that morning. "We are going to remove your Dad's ventilator soon," Clyde said and then was silent for a few moments, letting the words sink in.

"I have already spoken with your mother who understands. All of Kurt's vitals are failing. If you want to say goodbye, you should come and see him as soon as possible. The necessary papers have all been signed. If you come to the hospital, we'll try to make it possible for you to see your father through a glass window, only for a short while. We can't promise anything, so don't get your hopes up too high. It depends on what is happening at the time with the other patients, but we will try.

"I'm sure you understand why your mom cannot come; her health and the hospital's protocols make that impossible. I would suggest you come as soon as you are able."

His mother could not visit. It was an unfair system for an unfair time. Bo realized a short visit through glass was the best they could possibly do. It was a necessary policy to stem the virus. No visitors were allowed to visit COVID patients, especially not his mother who still suffered from the virus. Clyde would not have had to explain it. Hope had long run out.

Bo's father, Kurt, had become critically ill following his operation to replace a heart valve. It was a preventive procedure meant to give a higher quality of life, not kill him.

No one, certainly not his doctor, had expected Kurt to die. Bo had spoken to Dr. Hudson shortly after the surgical procedure when Hudson had been so confident. Everyone had assumed the surgery would be a success.

But no one knew that the surgeon was a COVID-19 carrier, least of all Dr. Hudson, when he operated on Kurt. Dr. Hudson had been tested for the virus the day before the surgery. It had registered negative that day, but not the next.

Kurt would never recover from the surgery. He would never know it was his doctor's unknown illness that caused his death. Kurt did not recover in time to be able to make final preparations. After only three weeks in the ICU, Kurt's lungs and heart were quickly giving out, new valve or not.

Dr. Hudson also had become critically ill. He would remain in ICU for two months, be on a ventilator for over a month; his return to his career in doubt.

Unfortunately, Clare, Bo's mother, had immediately contracted Covid from her husband. She was ill and in shock, but had not been hospitalized. Like all visitors, Kurt's wife was denied the privilege to watch over or visit her husband as he struggled day by day, hour by hour, minute by minute.

As soon as Bo got the call, he left immediately for the hospital, hopeful that he would be able to see Kurt before he died. Bo arrived at what was now an ICU waiting room. He was wearing a mask which made him feel very uncomfortable. Bo wondered; would his father even recognize him in a mask?

"I'm sorry," Clyde said, moments after greeting him. At first Bo thought he meant he would be denied a visit, but Clyde continued. "I thought your dad might make it. But things never got better. Only worse. He just didn't have a chance. There is nothing more we can do."

Bo too had been hopeful. He had kept thinking how strong his dad had always been and expected him to suddenly improve.

"I assume you still want to try to communicate with your Dad," Clyde said.

"Of course!" Bo responded. "I was afraid it would be impossible."

"We moved your father into a special room where you will be able to see him through a window. We are trying to make final visits available for patients and their loved ones. How successful we are depends on how busy we are. We can't promise. If he is awake, you will see your father through the window and communicate with him, I will go in first."

Clyde paused for a moment. "I assume it is still the family's wish to disconnect the ventilator when there is no more hope."

Bo nodded.

Clyde looked at him as if waiting for more of an answer.

"It is our wish and it is my father's wish," Bo managed. *Clyde must be aware his father had a long-standing DNR on file at the hospital,* he thought, *but apparently the nurse felt the need for Bo to verbalize a final assertion.*

"I need to change into the necessary PPE before I call you," Clyde explained. "Kurt will have an iPad and be able to see you on it. If he becomes conscious he may see you through the glass, but I doubt it. I will tell him you are here and wish to speak to him. Hopefully, he will be able to communicate. But remember, he is under sedation."

It was really going to happen, Bo thought. *"I am finally going to talk to my dad!* Only a week ago the doctor had said Kurt was too ill for anyone to visit. Now his Dad would not be able to see or hear Bo.

Clyde understood Bo's confusion and doubt. "Maybe he won't respond. But it is worth a try. We do what we can. Remember, you will have only a few minutes."

Bo nodded.

"Okay!" Clyde said. "Let's go! Follow me."

Clyde patted Bo on the back of his shoulder and together they left the waiting room.

Through heavy locked doors Bo followed Clyde onto what seemed a patient floor, moving deliberately past a sea of medical equipment, personal computers, and masked medical personnel assisting masked patients lying alone, one of them moaning, all in temporary make-shift areas. Apparently, they were awaiting admission and treatment.

After only a few more steps they stopped and Clyde showed Bo to a chair by a large window through which he could see Kurt, who was connected to a ventilator, resting on large mounds of pillows. "Sit here and wait while I change and go in. I'll see you in a few minutes." Clyde looked at Bo. "Try to relax. You will be fine."

Bo nodded.

Through the window, he saw his father, so alone in such a busy, otherwise chaotic area. Kurt, obviously struggling, was barely recognizable. He looked so helpless, so old. Could this man be his father who until a few months ago liked to play catch with him, who had been so strong, so able?

Bo shrunk down in the chair and waited.

Clyde was well rehearsed in donning PPE and it didn't take him much time to change clothing. When he appeared inside the room minutes later, he was covered with a floor-length gown, headgear, and a plastic face covering. Long gloves extended over his sleeves.

Clyde went over to Kurt who was not awake, studied him for a few seconds, looked at the patient monitor and then the ventilator, before he made eye contact with Bo, and nodded.

Bo watched Clyde carefully reading the machine's monitors. He seemed satisfied and sat down next to the patient. He nodded to Bo and made the necessary entries on the iPad.

Seconds later Bo's phone rang in the sick room.

"Hi, Dad. Can you hear me? It's Bo."

He could hear his father breathing hard, but nothing else.

Inside the room, Clyde repeated Bo's message to Kurt. "Kurt, It's your son, Bo. He wants to talk to you. Here, you can see him on the screen. He's right outside your room on the other side of the window. "

Kurt made no effort to speak but did open his eyelids.

"Do you want to talk to Bo, Kurt?" Clyde asked. "He came to see you. "

Kurt opened his eyes half-mast with a vacant look. Slowly, Kurt nodded his head.

Outside the window, Bo spoke slowly and clearly, "Hello. Hello Dad? It's Bo. It's Bo, Dad."

Kurt glanced at the window to see if he might find Bo there. Kurt's breathing was labored, but he made a throated grunting sound, which seemed to indicate recognition.

"Dad, I.... It is so good to see you. I am so sorry you are so ill. I want you to know-- I want you to know, I love you, Dad."

Bo waited for a few seconds. A strange guttural sound came from Kurt who was looking at the screen.

"Bo!" his father said "Bo!..... Where are you?"

"I--I'm right here on the other side of the window. I -- I came to say thank you, Dad. Thank you for all you've done for me, for all the great times we had, for everything you and mom made possible."

A look of pain crossed Kurt's face. He looked up from the screen to the window but did not seem to see his son Bo. Then Bo saw Kurt's lips move and thought he heard him say or form the word, "Ditto." It was a word his father would often use to indicate he thought the same thing or felt the same way.

"I love you, Dad." Bo said, his eyes filling with tears. "Dad, Mom can't come. She has the virus too, but she sent a message." Bo did not have a message, but he would invent one. "Mom says, she says 'Hi, Sweetheart' like she always does. Mom says to tell you that you are going to be fine. Wherever you go. Whatever you do. You will be fine. She misses you." Clyde cocked his head and raised his eyebrows, giving Bo a look that said-- hurry! Not much more time!

"We all miss you, especially George," Bo said, hurriedly. George was Kurt's German Shepherd. At the mention of George, Kurt smiled and made a sound of recognition. Clyde raised his eyebrows again, nodded his head toward the monitor, raised a hand in a "stop" sign, signifying it was time to end.

"I love you, Dad. We all love you...Blessings...Blessing on your way." Kurt suddenly shut his eyes. He was struggling to breathe. Their communication had ended. Bo buried his head in his sleeve. When he raised his head up again he saw Clyde gently lay his father's head back on the pillow. His father seemed to have gone to sleep, or perhaps into a coma. The iPad with a dark screen lay vacant on the bed. Bo took a last look at his father, gave Clyde a thumbs-up gesture and slowly stood up.

From inside the ICU unit, Clyde waved a soft goodbye. Bo pressed his hands together in prayerful thanks, bowed, and then made his way outside the hospital.

THE LAST LENTEN SERVICE - 2021

A lofty, sweet fragrance of cherry and apple blossoms filled the church garden playground, which along with a multi-colored swing set, cradled the worship area. Tonight, the Spirit Garden was in final preparations for the last Lenten service prior to Easter, 2021. People were gathering, carefully choosing their seats in chairs arranged according to a mix of social distancing restrictions--singles, couples and families with children.

Near the garden wall, an altar displayed a gold cross, fresh red roses, and an extra-large Bible. Off to the right side, a lectern and an electronic piano were plugged into the power grid to ensure proper sound for the evening service. A cool evening breeze breathed its gentle way through the garden. Pastor Maria was busy organizing her notes at the lectern so they wouldn't scatter. Shelly, the church organist, was arranging her music on the Yamaha electronic piano.

Several of the group's members were exuberant to be together in the garden, especially in such pleasant spring weather. Others sat quietly alone, six feet from a neighboring chair. The message was clear: COVID-19 restrictions are still intact. Masks covered facial expressions.

Bo Gordon had just driven into the church parking lot in the MG-TC he had inherited many years ago from his grandfather. This morning, he had come to church in his Granddad's ancient vanilla sports car because he was going to assist at the altar. Bo's wife Joellen, a third-grade teacher, would be coming later with their daughter Ava, a senior in the same high school where Bo taught chemistry. Andy, their son, was attending college in Texas.

Ever since his Dad died, Bo had been despondent; he felt like time was running out. He wished his children were more aware of how important the decisions they were making in their youth would determine so much of their future. In high school, Bo had wanted to be a doctor like his grandfather, but he wasn't encouraged in that direction, even by Granddad.

Now he wondered why. They had been so close. He supposed all jobs and professions had their disadvantages. Bo had liked, often loved teaching chemistry until the damn virus happened. Now he hated wearing a mask and hated teaching over the internet.

Bo just couldn't reach the kids when he couldn't look them in the eye, when he couldn't hear what they said, couldn't talk or listen to them. Having parked the car, Bo stepped into the gated church garden and was soon met by Hank, an older gentleman who had known Kurt and was serving as the evening's greeter.

"Hi there, Bo! Looks like we are going to have a good crowd," Hank said. "I think people are getting tired of Zoom, Zoom Zoom. You teach -- what? English? "

"No, Chemistry," Bo answered. He had taught high school chemistry in Albuquerque for 20 years now, and people still didn't remember what he taught.

Hank asked, "Still teaching over Zoom?"

"Oh, yes. I'm teaching both in person and by Zoom."

Hank turned to him and gave a serious but concerned look. "I'll bet you miss your Dad."

"Thanks," Bo answered. "Yes, I do," and he turned to get away from Hank. He didn't want to talk about his dad, about COVID-19, about his mother, or funerals, about dying or vaccines or anything else.

"How's it going?" Pastor Maria asked when Bo stepped up to be near her by the altar.

"Better," he answered with little enthusiasm but managed a small smile.

The pastor knew what he had been through. Pastor Maria, several of his friends, along with Joellen and the Men's Group, had helped Bo get through the difficult days after his father died.

Bo was very grateful and glad to be asked to be an assistant at tonight's last Lenten service. He took his seat near the altar. It was still 10 minutes before service; Bo wanted to sit quietly as people gathered.

Now lively chatter and greetings almost filled the garden, more like preparations for an Easter party than a Lenten service. People were glad to be out after months of isolation.

Shelly began playing the prelude. Sounds from Mozart escaped from the electronic piano, merged with the muffled chatter of church latecomers and a cacophony of street noises.

Another soft breeze blew gently around the blossoming fruit trees as Pastor Maria came to the lectern.

"Welcome everyone to our evening service in the Spirit Garden! What a gorgeous evening for our last Lenten service for 2021. We shall begin with a fitting old hymn which is dear to many of us. No. 341, "In the Garden."

Shelly played an introduction and people stood and sang out:

I come to the garden alone,
While the dew is still on the roses;
And the voice I hear, falling on my ear
The Son of God discloses
And He walks with me, and He talks with me,
And He tells me I am His own,
And the joys we share as we tarry there
None other has ever known.

Author: C Austin Miles

Following the hymn, Pastor Maria announced: "Let us all pray:

"Seeking peace in a time of stress, a time of suffering, illness, and pain, we pray for healing of all who suffer from COVID-19 and other diseases, and all who are burdened by loss, loneliness, or despair. Help each and every one of us to have hope!
"We give thanks for all the first responders and all who help heal the many patients who are ill. "Thank you for this beautiful evening when we can all gather. Amen."

Bo's mind wandered. *All those who help.* He thought of his father and was grateful for their last time together. He thought of what he wanted to do. For weeks now, Bo had felt almost a compulsion to quit his job. He wanted to get into the medical field where he belonged. He only wished he had known it earlier. Certainly, it was too late for him to become a doctor, but what about becoming a nurse, like Clyde?

He had even talked to Joellen about it, but she didn't seem to take him seriously. Maybe it was ridiculous at this point, unfair to his family.

Suddenly, Bo realized his attention had wavered. It was time for him to read the Bible lesson! People were waiting for him to come forward.

Uneasily, Bo Gordon stood up and moved toward the lectern, trying to clarify his mind. He was glad he had prepared the Bible, or he would have been a dead duck.

Looking out, he was glad to see Joellen in the back row. She was sitting with Ava, who was grinning at him. His daughter must have realized he was a bit unprepared for the moment.

Bo straightened his glasses and opened the Bible where he had marked the two parables he was to read. The lesson was exceptionally short, and he certainly didn't want to screw it up. One parable was only two sentences long and the other was only one sentence long.

He looked out once more, smiled, and began to read:

"The Parables of the Hidden Treasure" and "The Pearl of Great Price." Matthew Chapter 13, verses 44-46.

"The kingdom of heaven is like treasure hidden in a field. When a man found it, he hid it again, and then in his joy went and sold all he had and bought that field.

"Again, the kingdom of heaven is like a merchant looking for fine pearls. He found one of great

value, he went away and sold everything he had and bought it." Bo looked up. He was not accustomed to having such a short section to read. He paused for just a moment.

"The word of the Lord," he said and smiled.

"Thanks be to God," the congregation responded.

Bo returned to his chair. Pastor Maria stood, approached the microphone, turned toward Bo and smiled. "That was short and sweet."

Maria looked out at the congregation and began her sermon. "These two parables, while short, have important messages," she said, "especially for Lent.

"Several of you have 'given up' something for Lent, such as chocolate, or sweets. Or perhaps a habit such as repeatedly being late, which you wish to change, or you may be working on making some other positive change in your life, such as spending more time with your family. Lent is almost over. But it is never too late to give up something for a good reason.

"Often during Lent, we examine our lives and see how we are doing to fulfill our life's purposes. When this happens, we often realize we may need to take risks, or perhaps be patient, or likely give up something in order to attain or obtain what is most important to us.

"Let us look at the two simple parables and what they teach us. In The Parable of the Hidden Treasure, a man stumbles upon a treasure in a field. A real buried treasure! How amazing is that? First, he makes sure his new treasure is safe. He reburies it!"

"It must have been difficult not to just take it with him, but if he did so, it would be necessary to explain where he found it. If he purchases the land containing the treasure, it will then belong to him. It often takes patience to obtain what we want. This man fortunately is able to purchase the land, but he must give something up. He must sell almost all he owns."

"Clearly, this man is willing to give up all he has in order to have the treasure even though it involves some risk. Someone else could come upon the treasure before he owns the land.

"The second parable, The Pearl of Great Price, has a similar message. Imagine you are a connoisseur of beautiful pearls and for your entire life, you have searched for the most beautiful pearl in the world. You want the perfect pearl more than anything else,

"Finally, you find the perfect pearl! It is everything you ever wanted! Naturally, it costs a great deal of money. It can be yours, but you too must give up nearly everything you own, including all your other pearls and gems.

"In order for us to attain the goals we want most, we must do just as the merchant and the treasure-seeker did. First, we must know what we want and not let anything stand in our way of attaining it. The merchant had to sell everything he owned in order to buy the perfect pearl.

"The treasure-finder had to sell what he owned in order to purchase the land containing the treasure he had discovered. Both knew their priorities. Both were willing to let go of their existing possessions.

"The most common interpretation of the two parables is that the treasure and the perfect pearl are symbols of the Kingdom of God. This is so. Notice the materialistic nature of both stories!

"The merchant and the treasure-hunter/finder both recognize the importance of the material aspects of life. There is no reason that temporal and spiritual qualities of life should be in conflict. They should complement each other!

"Unfortunately, there are those who ruin their lives in a singular pursuit of material gains. They do not realize until it is too late that money is a magnificent servant, but a dangerous master! The Gospel condemns the love of money. It does not condemn money itself. Inordinate concern for money is the root of much that is evil!

"We can have almost anything we want if we are willing and able to pay for it. Or we can spend our *lives acquiring pebbles instead of pearls and find out too late we did not spend our limited time and strength pursuing what is important to us.*

"Tonight is a time to ask yourself, 'What more than anything do I want to have in my life?' It may be a particular job, a beautiful home, a trip somewhere, a relationship. You might happily discover you are spending time on what is most important to you! That's wonderful! Be thankful! If not, what is your pearl of great price? Can you give up what is needed in order to have it?

"The merchant was excited to have the opportunity to purchase the pearl of great price! How willing the treasure hunter was to wait until he could purchase the land!

"Do you have a buried treasure waiting for you to reclaim? Have you purchased the ground where it is buried? The merchant and the treasure-seeker cheerfully gave up what was needed in order to have what was most important to them.

"We can do likewise. Our choices determine our lives. If you want something important, give it your primary effort and attention. May God help each of us realize what is most important in our lives and have the courage to give up what is needed to joyfully attain what we ask for in life.

"Amen."

Pastor Maria's last statement was all Bo needed. Once he had wanted to go into medicine and he had done nothing to make it a reality. Now, Bo wanted to become a nurse. He wanted to help people, perhaps become a physician's assistant, or maybe work in an ICU.

Yes, he was 50 years old now, but this was a calling, something he had once thought existed only in a person's imagination. He knew in his heart that if he did not answer the call, he would regret it the rest of his life.

How would he explain it to Joellen, to Ava and his son Andy? His mother? Would they understand? Would they support him?

Bo wasn't sure, but he thought they would at least eventually, if not right away, understand and be supportive. But the family would have a financial gap that needed to be solved.

Could he go to nursing school part time? Find a part time job? Maybe become a substitute teacher or tutor? Somehow, they would find a way.

The entire family would need to give up luxuries they enjoyed for quite a while--vacations, frequently eating out, their plan to buy a new car.

His car!

There was something Bo could give up. His car! He loved his MG-TC more than anything else he owned. It was his identity; it symbolized his heritage. But he could let it go. His MG might get $30,000 - certainly not enough to cover his needs-- but it would help. And his family would realize how committed he was.

Yes, that was what he would give up for Lent-- or more precisely, give up for his and his family's future. Granddad's prized MG-TC. It was Bo's treasure.

Who wouldn't give up an MG-TC for a pearl of greater value? Bo prayed he would be cheerful about what it would cost him, just like the guys in the two parables. With God's help, he would have the strength to follow through on his new venture.

He thought his GrandDad would approve.

CHAPTER 10

Pentecost and The Parable of the Mustard Seed
Pastor Maria

"Welcome Home!" Pastor Maria proclaimed.

"It's great to be together again, *inside* the church after being bound such a long time by the pandemic! And this is Pentecost Sunday, the Birthday of the Christian Church! It is a wonderful synchronicity.

"For our opening Hymn, we will sing "O Day Full of Grace," Hymn 627. We will be singing it together for the first time in well over a year! It is truly a day full of grace!"

O day full of grace that now we see
appearing on earth's horizon,
bring light from our God that we may be
abundant in joy this season.
God, shine for us now in this dark place.
your name on our hearts emblazon.

God came to us then at Pentecost,
The spirit is now life revealing,
that we might no more in death by lost,
Its po'wr over us is dispelling.
This flame will the mark of sin efface
And bring to us all true healing.

(vs 1 and 4. N.F.S. Grundtvig; tr. composite Gerald Thomson)

Following the opening hymn, Pastor Maria stepped forward to begin the service: "Please join me in reciting the Prayer of the Day:

"Spirit of the Living God, we rejoice that You come to each and all of us who prepare for your great gifts. Help us, O God, to live each day, not just by idle words, but in ways that demonstrate we have within us your great gift of the Holy Spirit. Teach us to manifest the fruits of the Spirit: love, confidence and peace of mind, during life's most challenging times as well as in the best of times.
"Amen."

It was time to read the Gospel. Pastor Maria went to the podium:

"Our Gospel lesson for Pentecost is found in Acts, Chapter 2, vs 2-15. The Coming of the Holy Spirit.

"When the day of Pentecost had come, they were all together in one place. And suddenly from heaven there came a sound like the rush of a violent wind, and it filled the entire house where they were sitting. Divided tongues, as of fire, appeared among them, and a tongue rested on each of them.

"All of them were filled with the Holy Spirit and began to speak in other languages, as the Spirit gave them ability.

"Now there were devout Jews from every nation under heaven living in Jerusalem. And at this sound the crowd gathered and were bewildered, because each one heard them speaking in the native

language of each. Amazed and astonished, they asked, 'Are not all these who are speaking Galileans? And how is it that we hear, each of us, in our own native language? Parthians, Medes, Elamites, and residents of Mesopotamia, Judea and Cappadocia, Pontus and Asia, Phrygia and Pamphylia, Egypt and the parts of Libya belonging to Cyrene, and visitors from Rome, both Jews and proselytes, Cretans and Arabs—in our own languages we hear them speaking about God's deeds of power.'

"All were amazed and perplexed, saying to one another, 'What does this mean?' But others sneered and said, 'They are filled with new wine.'

"But Peter, standing with the eleven, raised his voice and addressed them, 'Men of Judea and all who live in Jerusalem, let this be known to you, and listen to what I say. Indeed, these are not drunk, as you suppose, for it is only nine o'clock in the morning.'

"The Gospel of the Lord."

"Although the story is very familiar, we do not know exactly what happened on the day of Pentecost. But we know from Acts that it was an extremely powerful event, involving wind, sound, and sight.

"The Holy Spirit was felt, heard, seen by all and individually communicated to an incredibly wide diversity of gathered people who were able to hear the *message spoken in their native language. This was a long time before technology arrived, and without very advanced technology, would still be impossible.*

"Pentecost is the fulfillment of the promise that fulfills Jesus' last words to his disciples: 'It is not for you to know times or seasons which the Father has fixed by his own authority. But you shall receive power when the Holy Spirit has come upon you: and you shall be my witnesses in Jerusalem and in all Judea and Samaria and to the ends of the earth.'

"Without this dramatic, intense spirit visitation, the disciples and the other followers of Jesus would not have had the energy, confidence, inspiration, power, and faith to spread the word throughout the ancient world. This is why Pentecost is known as the birthday of the Christian Church.

"Pentecost changes the ministry of Jesus from past memories that would likely have been lost, to a vibrant present experience.

"To experience Pentecost is to experience power. The Holy Spirit is power, an active power within our inner life.

"Pentecost made Christmas and Easter something to experience and celebrate rather than something that happened over 2,000 years ago. Unlike Christmas or Easter, Pentecost is the one major Christian holiday which is not celebrated in the secular world.

"Christmas celebrates Jesus' birth. It is also a major secular, legal holiday with no mail service, celebrated by virtually everyone.

"Christmas is celebrated about the same time as the winter solstice which was intentional; it is the busiest time of the year and has huge economic consequences. It is a time for parties, family gatherings, concerts, school programs, gift giving, decorating, vacations and traveling.

"At Easter, Christians celebrate the resurrection of Jesus. Easter is also a popular time in secular society, a time for children to hunt for Easter eggs, find candy in their Easter baskets, and greet Easter bunnies.

"Without Pentecost, it is unlikely we would have either Christmas or Easter to celebrate.

"Pentecost took place 50 days after Easter; it is celebrated seven weeks after Easter in order for Pentecost to be observed on a Sunday. Unlike Easter or Christmas, it is unnoticed or ignored in the secular world.

"How do you think secular society would celebrate Pentecost if they did commemorate the event? Santa Claus and the Easter Bunny represent the secular holidays. How might we represent secular society at Pentecost?

"One can imagine and speculate. Since Pentecost is about power, albeit spiritual power, a giant fire-breathing dragon might be used. Fireworks and homemade rocket launchings are a possibility or even having a live NASA rocket event?

"Gifts given for a secular Pentecost might inspire power roller skates or jet-propulsion-driven toy cars.

"Easter and Christmas always included special ethnic or traditional meals. A Pentecostal menu might include exotic green power salads, powerful energy or ultra healthy vitamin drinks.

"While imaginative, none of these ideas capture Pentecost, which is a mystical experience. Pentecost doesn't lend itself to ordinary entertainment.

"Pentecost is not man-made. Christians usually do not entertain family or friends at Pentecost. They don't give or receive gifts, decorate their home or have parties.

"Pentecost is significant. It is a time to give thanks for the Holy Spirit's descension on the day of Pentecost and the incredible mystical power the Holy Spirit event provided, with effects which have continued for over 2000 years and persist today.

"At Pentecost the Holy Spirit transmits power to people who need it. Sometimes it is transmitted to

groups like the first Pentecost and at other times to individuals. The Holy Spirit empowers people who face major challenges.

"They are able to become unafraid.

"The book of Acts is in sharp contrast to people's response to the resurrection according to Mark, Chapter 16, v8: 'And they went out and fled from the tomb; for trembling and astonishment had come upon them, and they said nothing to any one, for they were afraid.'

"Through Pentecost, faith based on memories, became current, and remained current.

"Jesus' birth took place in a small corner of the world to what seemed ordinary people. That Mary had a baby was not important news at the time. The life, death and resurrection of Jesus was also not international news when it occurred.

"From humble beginnings Christianity became the world's largest religion. In 2020, about one third, of the world's population, were Christian or 2.382 billion people. The world's Christian population is expected to grow to 2.9 billion by 2050.

"The story of the growth of Christianity is like the Parable of the Mustard Seed. Chapter 13: VS 31- 32. The kingdom of heaven is like a mustard seed, which a man took and planted in his field. Though it is the smallest of all seeds, yet when it grows, it is the

largest of garden plants and becomes a tree, so that the birds come and perch in its branches.'

"While the parable of the Mustard Seed is an excellent analogy of the incredible growth of the Christian Church, the passage is really about the growth of "The Kingdom of God."

"The Christian Church is an earthly institution, comprising numerous churches and various denominations which share the belief in the divinity of Jesus. It is both a vehicle and a vessel for The Holy Spirit. However, the Kingdom of God is a spiritual entity, which is not physical.

"Jesus uses the mustard seed metaphor in two other instances in the Bible. From Matthew 17:20: 'For truly I tell you, if you have faith the size of a mustard seed, you will say to this mountain, 'Move from here to there,' and it will move; and nothing will be impossible for you.'

"And in Luke 17:6: 'If you had faith the size of a mustard seed, you could say to this mulberry tree, 'Be uprooted and planted in the sea, and it would obey you.'

"The concept of having the faith of a mustard seed is somewhat puzzling because we humans are quite different from mustard seeds. Our creator endowed us with minds as well as hearts. We are meant to use them, just as the mustard seed uses its resources.

"It is necessary to listen carefully to our hearts and minds when we are challenged. To move mountains, we must have faith --faith like a mustard seed!

"The mustard seed does not grow from a seed to a large tree in an instant. Faith grows and goes through different stages, just as the mustard seed grows from out of the ground to sprout, to grow to a bush-like plant to finally a tree! It does not grow in a flash! Faith takes root, spouts, and gradually grows until it too serves God's creatures.

"Pentecost was a sudden, dramatic event. The Holy Spirit descended; seeds of faith are planted, sprout and grow. Both are acts of God's grace.

"Faith like the mustard seed can enable us to do what seems humanly impossible. When we ask for the Holy Spirit to help us, we ask for power in our inner lives.

"But be careful what you pray for because you are asking for change, and change is often difficult. If you pray for patience, you may find yourself in a situation where you will need to learn patience; it will not be given in a single package.

"'Does God always answer prayers?' you might ask.
"Whatever happens is very likely an answer. There are several possibilities.

"What you request may occur at a time or in a way that is unexpected.

"If not aligned with God's will, it likely won't happen.

"God may say 'no' if it is an unworthy purpose.

"You may come to realize that what you wanted is not what is needed, or even that it is not what you really wanted after all.

"Let your awareness be your answer. Do not be discouraged or doubtful.

"For lifetimes after lifetimes, The Holy Spirit has empowered people, provided them with divine power to accomplish human endeavors in the most difficult of circumstances with incredible results often seen as impossible.

"You may have heard an athlete say, 'I was carried by something outside of myself.' All his resources had been used-- but something else helped.

"Ask yourself, 'What is my life purpose and how am I doing?'
'What do I want? What is my need for power?'

"Today, right now, in celebration of Pentecost we are going to have a few minutes of silence. Use this time for prayer or simply meditate or sit silently and listen to what God, or your soul, tells you. It is up to you!

"If today you are facing a great challenge or many challenges, ask for help from the Holy Spirit.

"COVID-19 has taught us a lot about our priorities and led us to make important changes. For this, we are deeply thankful. It is also true that all have suffered. Some of you have lost family members and other people you dearly loved.

"This has been a year of unprecedented chaos--personal isolation, economic problems, loss of income, failure of businesses, education conflicts, problems related to climate change, racial injustice, and deep political divisions challenging our democracy. We pray for guidance to do God's will, to find our way each and every day.

"Today we are celebrating what we hope is the beginning of the end of this extremely dangerous virus. Life is becoming closer to 'normal.' Our children will be returning to school! Travel is resuming. Businesses are fully resuming. Restaurants are returning to full or at least a greater capacity.

"We are together here--again-- inside in our church! For all this and much more, we give our deep, deep thanks to God!

"We do not know the future of this virus. We do not know if this is simply a pause. What happens tomorrow, in the next few weeks or next few years is unknown.

"Right now, together, let us take a few minutes to thank God for all we have been given, and ask for whatever you need for support as we face the coming days together.

"Remember, we need not fear. The opposite of fear is love. Let us eliminate our fear and exponentially increase our love for each and everyone.

"The word of our Lord."

"Thanks be to God." responded the Congregation.

Pastor Maria moved away from the pulpit and faced the congregation in front of the altar.

"Let us now pray individually, and then hold five minutes of silence for the lives of our loved ones whom we mourn, especially those whose lives ended this past year. When our period of silence is complete, I will lead us in a group prayer. Let us begin:

"Dear God, hear our prayers this day and hold us in the loving arms of faith, hope, love, grace and truth..."

CHAPTER 11

Prayers in the Pandemic

(Dan, Consuela, Nikia; Michael, Gloria, Andy, Chelsea, Charlie; Alicia, Becky, Romeo, Ian; Sue Ellen, Jack, Stacey; Rita, Carl, Leah, Haim; Kaitlin; Robbie, Robert; Edith, Joel, and Bo.)

Throughout the sanctuary, people sat quietly. Some bowed their heads; many closed their eyes. A baby modestly protested. Only God and the angels heard the petitions.

Dan, Consuela and Nikia were sitting in the third row from the back.

Consuela: Thank you God that the danger from COVID-19 is much less, and that none in our family became ill! Thank you that our beloved Silver Sands is still going strong! Bless all our customers who have supported us. We are so dependent on them. And thank you to our staff. We are so grateful for the many who helped us when things were really tough and are still with us. Please help us to keep going, and that we not have a relapse! Thank you for our customers who kept supporting us! Please let us never let them down. Bless our trip to Belize! I am so grateful we can go! Keep us safe. Help my parents to accept Dan. Help Dan to understand and love my parents! I miss them so much. I want Nikia to be close and to understand them. I know they will love her. Help them understand her. Please help Dan not to worry so much. Help us keep going! Help us to remain strong. Amen."

Dan: "Thank you for getting us through the virus by the skin of our teeth! Help this country and the entire world recover from COVID-19. Continue to help us keep our restaurants going; give us the strength to handle whatever happens to Silver Sands. Thank you for all the blessings you have given us. Thank you for Consuela! We are so fortunate to have each other. Give me the patience to be a better father to Nikia. Bless us all! Thank you! Thank you! In Jesus' name. Amen."

Nikia: "I don't know what to pray for. I'll just sit here and be quiet. If I did pray, I'd ask to see my father when we get to Belize. I have never known him. Yes, I pray to meet and see my father. And that he is a good person. Amen."

Michael: "Thank you, dear God, Thank you for AA. Help me continue to live 24 hours at a time. Help me to learn how to have faith like a mustard seed. I am lonely. I pray that I can meet someone new in my life. I would like to have a partner, someone with whom I can share my life. Give me the strength to have a new relationship and to keep it! Help me to love again. Help me keep sober. It is not as difficult as I thought it would be. Do not let me fail. Help me to never let my guard down. Thank you for Gloria and my sponsor. Both of them believe in me. Help me to believe in myself more than I do. Help me to be my own best friend. I am so thankful for my job and my new life here. Bless AA and all my friends. Help those who have fallen away. Give them hope and new strength. Amen."

Gloria: (Sitting with Michael and their children, Chelsea and Charlie, and her husband Andy.) "Thank you, Holy Spirit, for bringing us here this morning. I am so glad we have come. I feel like we belong here which is not what I thought I would feel. Thank you for helping Michael--and for helping me! Increase my faith in other people, especially Andy. Help me to honor and love him, to not try to change him, and not try to change Michael. Thank you Chelsea and Charlie. Teach me to be more patient with them. Help me enjoy them more, to know what is best for them, and not to worry so much. Help us have more fun together. Help me not to worry so much and to love myself more. Amen."

Andy: "A few minutes more. Just a few minutes. Help me get through this service."

Alicia: (Sitting next to her grandson Ian holding a small plastic bag half full of the Cheerios she had just given him.) "Thank you, God, for the new relationship I have with my daughter and her husband. We are getting along so well now. Thank you for helping us change. Thank you for my beautiful grandson. And my daughter! Holy Spirit, help me find a retirement home that I like and where I can make a new life. Help me find a place close enough to visit my family often and a church where I am comfortable. Help me to make a good life and feel at home here. Amen."

Becky: "Thank you for having my mother here. It is a lot easier than when she was so far away. Thank you that she and Ian get along so well. Keep them safe. Thank you for our family. We are more a family than we have ever been. Help my mother to get accustomed to her new life here. In Jesus name, I pray. Amen."

Ian: "Dear Jesus and God, Help my Grandma. She is very nice to me. Help me get a dog. I will take good care of it. Thank you! Amen."

Sue Ellen: "Dear Jesus, I need your help! I am pregnant. I think I am-- I know I am. Please help me handle my pregnancy without being crazy like I was when I was expecting Stacey. Help Jack and I prepare for a baby and help us be wonderful parents to Stacey and the baby! Keep us forever close to each other. Help Stacey to accept and care for a brother or sister. I don't want her to ever feel left out. I would like a boy. A girl is okay, but I would really like a boy. Oh, I guess it might be too late to ask. Either way. We will love whatever you send! Thy will be done! Oh, thank you, God! I am so happy! Amen."

Jack: "Thank you and thanks to everyone who helped make COVID-19 lose its grip, to manage it, or even go away. Keep it away, please! Thank you for the millions of vaccinations. I didn't think it would ever be over! Help me to understand those who keep refusing help, those who won't get vaccinated or wear masks. I don't understand them. I worry about Stacey. She is too young to be vaccinated. If anything happened to her, Sue Ellen would go crazy. Watch over her; protect her! Watch over all of us. Help us be kinder to one another.

Bless Sue Ellen and keep her as beautiful and sweet as she is! And bless the new addition-- Help me to be a really good dad and the best husband ever! Amen."

Rita: "Dear God, Dear Holy Spirit, So much has changed. Bless all of us. I am very thankful that Carl is feeling so much better about Leah's marriage. I knew she wouldn't change her mind. Help us to have a blessed wedding for her. Help us to honor both Christian and Muslim customs at their wedding. Help Carl and I to open our hearts wider and truly accept Haim. He is Leah's choice. Help Carl and I see Haim as Leah sees him, and learn more about him, his family, and his religion. Help us to love them and support their marriage. I pray I can help out again in a food bank. Help all the hungry people who are hungry and need food, especially the children. In Jesus' name. Amen."

Carl: "Forgive me for hurting my daughter. Return us to the trust and belief we once had in each other. Help me to see the strength and goodness in Haim and to have faith in my daughter's belief in him. Help me to talk less and listen more, especially whenever I am with Leah. Bless us all!"

Leah: "Thank you, God, that Mom and Dad are finally accepting that I will marry Haim. I was afraid their rejection would go on forever. It would have been terrible to handle if it continued. I want all of us to care for each other.

"Help Haim and I to create a marriage that is full of love-- not only for just Haim and I, but for all of us.

"I am so happy we are all together here in our family pew. I am so glad. Thank you, God!

"Help us become a united family.

"Praise be to God! Jesus, be with each and all of us every day.

"Amen."

Haim: "O Allah, heal Your servant who is suffering from illness. Restore my dear father to health and strength. I am so worried about him. Grant patience to Leah and I, and to her family and mine to get to know and love each other. Fill our hearts and minds with peace.

"Aameen"

Kaitlin: "Dear God, I pray for Neil; I pray for myself. I miss Neil so much. The time we had together was the best time of my life. I should thank you for the time we had together, but I miss him too much! Help me to... to believe in a future without him.

"Sometimes I just want to join him! I was doing so well. I thought I had accepted what happened. But I ...I am angry, angry at Neil for not being more careful, for not asking me to go skiing with him, for ruining my life when he ended his! I don't think I can love anyone else again, not like I loved him!

"Why didn't you save him, God? You could have let him know he shouldn't go down that mountain. He would have listened to you. He would have! He talked to you, God. Why didn't you help him when he needed you? Why didn't you prevent him from going down that unsafe mountain?

"You could have saved him, God! Why didn't you? Why didn't you? (She begins to quietly sob.)

"Sorry, God. I'm sorry. Forgive me. I'm just having a hard time. Please help me accept what happened.

"Comfort Neil's mother and father, his sister and brother. We are all heartbroken. Help me, help each of us to find peace.

"If I could just know he is okay.

"Could...could you have Neil send me a sign, let me know he is okay?

"Climate Change. Is that the problem? It was too warm the day of the avalanche! Was it because of climate change that you let this happen? Do you want us to do more about climate change?

"Neil was always doing his best! He recycled everything. We...he was going to get an electric car! Now it's too late. We won't ever have a car together. God, it's not fair!

"Could you at least send more rain? It is so dry here in Albuquerque. The Rio Grande is drying up!

"Bless Neil wherever he is. And bless Mother Earth.

"Oh, God, help me to have faith again. Help me to love again. A little more courage would help me a lot. Or faith. Maybe--one small mustard seed?

"Amen."

Robbie: "Help me decide if I should major in Criminal Justice. Help me to know if it is the best path for me to follow. I just don't know. It is what I want to do-- but I don't know for sure. Help me to be more sure.

"Holy Spirit, take away some of people's powerful weapons. Guns! It is making everything worse. Help us to make new laws, so there aren't so many mass shootings. I'm afraid of what's going to happen if things get worse. I want to do something to help. Show me the way.

"And please bring football back.

"Amen."

Robert Ackermann II: "Oh Lord, it is so good to be here. I haven't been here for a long time. Golf, you know. I'll try to come more often.

"Thank you for helping me work with my son. Thank you for telling me to listen. I know you're right. And I am beginning to have more confidence in him. Thank you for raising him up the way he is. I guess we have problems, but with your help, I know he will do okay. He might even do great things. Thank you! Thank you for our lives."

Edith: "Dear God, thank you for giving us hope for the future. I pray for Congress to pass a bill -- HR1 or whatever-- to protect the right to vote. I am afraid of what is happening. So many people are being left behind. Help people to see hypocrisy where it exists--to be aware when truths are covered up by lies.

"Show those who choose to ignore doing what they know is right. Help them to be brave, to listen to others and to their own souls, to follow the truth, and to do what they know is right. Give them the courage to be authentic. Help me to love those who disagree with me.

"Help us to embrace equality for everyone! Bless Joel! I don't think it is going to work out between us. We're too different. Help me see him more as a person. Help me to accept myself and that we can become good friends. Amen."

Joel: "My heart is heavy because I supported President Barnum and believed in him. The insurrection in the capital and trying to stop election results changed my opinion of him. Forgive me for not seeing this side of him sooner.

"I pray for the capital policemen who died in the January insurrection of the capital and for those who are still working there. Help those who believed Barnum, who thought they were patriots, and who now must live with their misunderstanding and wrongful acts. Enable all of us to accept the truth when it is difficult and embarrasses us because of our acceptance.

"Help me to forgive those who purposely misled and continue misleading people for purely selfish reasons. I don't feel I can trust anyone. I don't want to have anything to do with politics for a long time. Help me to find the truth.

"In Jesus name, I pray,

"Amen."

Bo: "Thank you for the time I had with Dad before he died. It meant so much. I give thanks that I sold my car quickly and for a better price than I expected! Please help Mom to fully recover. She still is not well. Give me the faith of a mustard seed to fulfill my dream to be a nurse.

"Help my family accept our new way of life, in spite of the difficulties and differences it will make. Help me to study well and become an excellent nurse.

"Bless my application to nursing school. Help me be an excellent nurse who truly helps the people I care for.

"In Jesus' name, I pray.

"Amen."

Pastor Maria returned to the microphone:

"Today, we give thanks for the birth, life, passion and resurrection of Jesus Christ and for sending us the Holy Spirit at Pentecost.

"We give thanks for the many visitations of the Spirit throughout history which continue today in ways we do not always realize.

"We give thanks to all the hearts and souls who are with us and help us on our life journeys. We are grateful for the countless incredible blessings we have received.

"Meeting the challenges is what has strengthened us. Now we face an unknown and possibly a difficult future.

"This has been a year of unprecedented chaos--personal isolation, economic problems, loss of income, failure of businesses, education conflicts, problems related to climate change, racial injustice, deep political divisions challenging our democracy. We pray for guidance to always do God's will, finding our way each and every day.

"We ask for blessings and wisdom as we face many challenges including the mistrust and continual pandemic concerns.

*"Help us to know the true power of Christ's Consciousness and Pentecostal power. Help us to exponentially increase love among all humanity.
In Jesus name,*

Amen."

"We will close by singing, "God Be with You Till We Meet Again." It is page 536 in your hymn book."

God Be with you Till We Meet Again
by good counsels guide, uphold you,
With a shepherd's care enfold you:
God be with you till we meet again.

Refrain:

Till we meet, till we meet,
till we meet at Jesus' feet.
Till we meet, till we meet,
God be with you till we meet again.
(Text: Jeremiah E. Rankin)

Amen.

Church service ends.

Years pass:

2021

2022

2023

2024

A new paradigm begins to be noticed.

Chapter 12

THE NEW PARADIGM

Love, Oneness, Truth, Soul, Light, Gratitude, Compassion, Intuition, Individuality, Community, Service, Equality, Justice, Cooperation, Balance.

Unusual and exciting changes are being heralded as we begin the second quarter of the new century-- 2025.

The most painful aspects of COVID-19 seem to be behind us. We do not know for certain. Many people are still becoming ill; some are dying. Millions of lives have been changed forever caused by the virus and its puzzling, often untreatable, long-term effects. The high drama of the pandemic has lessened but is well remembered by those who are or were deeply affected by the virus. Thousands of people are becoming vaccinated, but new cases continue.

Most of those who become ill with COVID-19 in spite of being vaccinated do not become as seriously ill. Many still refuse vaccinations. Hospitalizations and deaths are less frequent for the vaccinated, but COVID-19 sometimes returns to patients even two or three times. While there are more light cases, patients can suffer from severe pain in the throat, stomach problems, extreme weakness, inability to taste food and other health problems from mild colds to difficulty breathing or even pneumonia. Long-term effects for some patients remain a mystery.

Our world is not the same. The wounds of political unrest continue; divisions are deep. Most people tend to be committed to their original viewpoints for preventing or treating COVID-19 with remarkably few people changing their minds.

What is most surprising is the effect COVID-19 has had on our politics, culture and social life. I recall how excited we were at the prospect of COVID-19 ending-- finally becoming able to be in crowds again-- go to movies, and parties, not wear masks at events, attend church and other group meetings, go out to dinner, shop, or visit others. Ironically, now that we can get together more freely, many of us choose to go less than before COVID-19; many people rarely attend events they had greatly missed.

The aftereffects of the virus have been the opposite of what many expected. We became more accustomed to staying home. Life is easier without the melodrama of attending certain events. Except for going to sports events where audiences are emotionally charged, crowds are now smaller. Movies and live entertainment programs are just beginning to have larger attendance. This is not so with many vacation areas and national parks which are very popular. Nonetheless, it is amazing how satisfied we became to attend meetings via Zoom, or simply just stay home. Why has so much changed?

We are in a new era, one which is being revealed. What is happening to us is unexpected. We are gradually being introduced to--or even becoming more enlightened about life itself. We have turned inward rather than outward. We look more to ourselves, our families, and those close to us rather than to outside activities. We have realized how interdependent we are, and how reliant on family and friends who can help us. We are more thankful and more willing to assist them.

The parables in this book illustrate some of what happened to people during the Pandemic and what they learned from it. COVID-19 caused many of us to "go to a far country" as is described in the parable of "The Prodigal Son." (It could also be for prodigal daughters.) It is necessary to spend time away from one's usual environment or to protest in order to find out who one really is, and what is most important. We need to "come to ourselves," and we may find that in doing so we "suffer" -- we realize our mistakes or weaknesses before we can come to a new understanding of what we want to do and be in our lives. Then we can "come home."

Think of "The Pearl of Great Price" or "The Hidden Treasure." We must give our whole selves to what is most important to us. (Or we may learn that what we once thought was most important is no longer the case.) We are finding out what is of most importance to our selfhood (our souls), including changing opinions about material values, accomplishments, reputation, and spirituality. That is important to know.

In the story of "The Foolish Bridesmaids," we see the power of timing. A wonderful opportunity will not always be available. We need to be open to what is offered when it is available and not give our power (oil) away. We need to honor and protect our special light-- our gifts-- and use them in a respectful way.

"Laborers in the Vineyard," reminds us that the natural laws of life on earth are rarely changeable. (Sometimes miracles occur in the natural world, but seldom.) Nature's laws provide stability and do not bend to willfulness. We learn to respect as well as be comforted by nature.

"New Patches on Old Garment" carries a major theme for the New Paradigm. There are times when we need something entirely new to make the necessary changes. This is not a time to patch many world problems. Patches will not make the necessary difference! We cannot simply patch up the old, making a few improvements here and there. This is not a matter of temporarily fulfilling overdue obligations or pleasing egos. No, we need some completely new approaches to make huge, magnificent changes.

We are faced with not only thinking about essential equality as a possibility but rather truly realizing its truth within our hearts. We need to love every person in our lives and see the divinity in every individual we meet and in ourselves. All of us come from the same source.

There is a realization in our world today that neither capitalism nor socialism nor dictatorships are meeting the needs of humanity. Axel Kildegaard quotes Dean Alchin of Wales, quoting the Bishop of Coventry in England. "Unless we can find a third way, collaborative and interdependent, especially for the weakest and the poorest, we shall never begin to discover a more satisfying way of life."

(Church and Life, Vol. LVIII, Number 4, April 15, 1999)

The New Paradigm is an indication that a new more "satisfying way of life" may be coming. What are some of the positive aspects the COVID-19 pandemic brought to our attention?

We learned that most Americans have come to respect the importance of help and support available from other people, the dearness of family, and the need for community. We need each other! We need time with ourselves to reflect on who we are and what we are about. The pandemic made us realize how quickly life can change.

We are less likely to want to live with too many distractions. For many people, materialism is no longer the primary focus. Many people have discovered that power and wealth are not immune from disaster. Protection of our materialistic ways, accomplishments and acquisitions is limited by their own reality.

Our basic nature has changed. Perhaps more than any other time we see ourselves as existential beings rather than objects with various automatic responses. We have come to realize we create our own lives. Religion, culture, government, education, history, fortune, current events, and even our DNA, affect us, but we are the prime creators of their effects on our hearts and souls, our human lives.

Climate change is happening and will continue. Time is getting very short! Poverty and the cost of living have increased, but it is also true that power and wealth are less relevant than before the pandemic. Personal success is being redefined. Working hard is important, but overworking, overspending, focusing on busyness or even constant entertainment is a drag. Recognition is overvalued. We need more "downtime" to bring our spirits up.

The power of superpowers and superwealth continues but is no longer unshakable. Can the world ever change? Greed, selfishness, super materialism, and unethical lies continue, but no longer dominate our culture. Becoming fearless is unattainable for those who rely exclusively on power and might,

Each of us must go inside our hearts and souls to find our divinity connections. It is where we find truth and glory. As we turn inward, we become closer to the outside. This is not about tolerating each other or approving of each other. It is about loving one another. LOVE! This is all about love!

LOVE

Jesus: "I say unto you, Love your enemies, bless them that curse you, do good to them that hate you, and pray for them which despitefully use you, and persecute you." (Matthew 5:43–44)

Loving one's enemies is not only a concept. It is a way to be human. What a way to live! It is not that difficult. There is such a thing as forgiveness of others and forgiveness of self. We can learn to use discernment rather than judgment. Discernment is a mental exercise of analyzing or describing what is faulty and how it can be improved. It is not about judgment and punishment, it is about accountability.

Love and Fear are the two most powerful forces on Planet Earth. Love is the basis of good on Earth. Fear is strong, counteracts joy, attracts lies, adds harmful stress, resists truth and prevents solutions from occurring. The only good use of fear is to prevent specific dangers. You, yourself, may have done many wrongs, even worse ones than actions you have found unforgivable. Love is much more powerful than fear. We can transform fear by adding more love to whatever challenges we face.

MORE ABOUT LOVE

Love is what this is all about. Once, while still handling dualisms, I examined the gift of loving others. I became aware that often, for no reason, I had a critical thought about someone-- instead of loving them! I was amazed and disappointed in myself. I noticed that when I saw a friend or colleague a judgment would often come up. I was critical of an outfit someone wore, or manner they had, or even a haircut, none of which was my business. What kind of person was I to feel disapproval about a person who wasn't doing anything wrong or hurting others? I obviously was affected by some old paradigms, love mixed up by judgement. I certainly wasn't being loving. I wasn't discerning. I was being dualistic, critical-- I liked this, and I didn't like that. I was making judgments.

I am better than that! I decided to send love toward someone for whom I felt criticism. Almost immediately, I realized something was still not right -- I was sending thoughts of love. I wasn't sending them my love. I was sending them thoughts -- not love itself.

So, I tried again. This time I felt the love I had for them and sent some of it! LOVE---to several friends/ acquaintances, one at a time. Each was a love blessing. Each time I LOVED THEM, I sensed they received it and were nourished. What a difference!

Now, instead of sending thoughts of love, I send a deep personal sincere love. It makes all the difference.

While love and fear are the two most powerful forces on earth, love is the most powerful. Love is the basis of good on earth. We overcome fear with love. We eliminate our fear by choosing love. Love is what makes us divine. We recognize the divinity in each of us as the primary oneness we share. We do not fear or hate anyone. Realizing and recognizing the divinity in every single person we know or meet stirs love, understanding and compassion in us.

What is Love? Love is God. As human beings we are partly God; we are each and all divine beings. Love is energy. Love is healing energy. We are beings composed of light and radiant with love.

Love deeply. Love yourself. Love Jesus. Love Gaia. Love God. Love others.

It is extremely important that we love ourselves. This is not about being egotistical (self-centered) with no or little regard for others. Without loving and accepting ourselves we cannot accept and love others as divine human beings. Care to love and accept the me in you that needs love the most. When needed, ask for help for loving yourself, others, God, Gaia. Everyone!

REVELATION

"Revelation," the last book of the Christian Bible, was authored by St. John and includes his dramatic vision. "Revelation" is considered an ancient prediction of an end time or major transition in our world. It has a heavily symbolic prediction that gets at the heart of how this complex world may end. Interpretations by philosophers, astrologers, and scientists in various parts of the world are controversial but are generally convinced that major changes are likely to occur. Many books and videos describe our future. Check out: YouTube for the latest predictions.

The book, "Revelation," is usually interpreted as an unmistakable presentation of a dualistic "Old Paradigm" universe-- good vs bad. "Revelation" is often seen as a preview of the end of the world and it generates fear. Do we have an angry violent God who takes revenge? For many the answers and the teachings are terrifying.

SELF–DISCOVERY AS THE NEW JERUSALEM

The news is not good, at least at first consideration. We have free will. Whether the New Paradigm leads us to enlightenment or only to an age of hell and suffering could be up to us. Major changes seem inevitable, but the future likely depends on us.

The book "Revelation" is interpreted very differently by various scholars. I am partial to Peter Lorie's interpretations from his book, "Revelation, St. John the Divine's Prophecies for the Apocalypse and Beyond" (Simon and Schuster, 1994).

Lorie defines the "New Jerusalem" not geographically, but rather as the process of self-discovery, wherein a new world emerges, and a thousand years of peace is predicted. Whatever happens, it seems for the rest of this century and possibly into additional centuries, we earthlings can expect cataclysmic difficulties before there is beauty, fulfillment, transformations and enlightenment.

Countless prophecies indicate earthly calamities: dehydration, volcanic eruptions, famine, social unrest, destabilizing conflict, war, etc. How much suffering and how long it lasts are unknown.

"Beloved, do not forget this one thing, that with the Lord one day is as a thousand years, and a thousand years are as one day." 2 Peter. 3-8.

The New Jerusalem in the "Book of Revelation" could be a symbol of a new way of looking and seeing. To know oneself is to become more familiar with what you call your soul or your higher self, your guide, your angel, or your true self. It is what continues when you die. Communication with the true self deeply enriches life.

FEMININE AND MASCULINE ENERGIES

According to Peter Lorie in his book, "Revelation, St John The Divine Prophecies for the Apocalypse and Beyond," the most important single prediction in the New Paradigm is the greater presence of women as a source of power in the world.

The greater presence of women is a statistical sign of the presence of the New Divine Feminine Energy-- one which merges and balances masculine and feminine energy. It can be found in both males and females--wherever feminine and masculine energy are balanced. All women and all men possess both feminine and masculine energy. Many women have a great deal of masculine energy; many men have a wide range of characteristics of feminine energy. Energy is the source of our power. We are becoming more able to balance these two different energies.

What is the difference between feminine energy and masculine energy?

For thousands of years, history has been dominated by masculine energy. We are now having a merger of the energies. Masculine energy has dominated societies because male bodies statistically are stronger than female bodies. Men have had physical power over women for many civilizations, century after century.

What are some common characteristics of feminine energy? It is more difficult to define than is anticipated, but historically, typical feminine energies have been signified by physical weakness, gentleness, emotions, and artistic abilities. Typical male energies are seen as wielding power, displaying restricted emotions, physical and mental ability and discipline.

What is now celebrated as The New Divine Feminine Energy is a balance of both male and female energies. As a species, we are ready for changes is much needed.

The New Divine Feminine Energy is for both men and women and is increasingly becoming stronger. Women are having new roles of power throughout society. Women utilizing masculine power to be effective are not any more successful than their masculine predecessors. Men and women must use oneness rather than dualism to make progress.

Physical punishment or cruelty is no longer considered a sign of power. The power of men or women is primarily due to their personal talents and resources, training, education, experiences, communication skills and personal "know-how".

Both female and male genders seek to possess and use energies that are intentionally helpful, practical, and familiar. Neither men nor women of character support lies or fear as keys to expressing their power.

The increase of The New Divine Feminine Energy on planet earth is a cosmic event and a balance of female and male energy is what is most important. It is part of the divine plan. Love and hope, goodness and light, intelligence, powerful solutions, and caring for one another are practical, attractive options for being successful!

THE RETURN OF RELIGIOUSNESS

Peter Lorie's second prediction in the New Paradigm is: "The return of religiousness," His use of the word "religiousness" does not mean becoming more engaged with old-time religions. Like several other prophets, he writes of a transformation of organized social religions.

Lorie defines "religiousness" as something human nature needs as much as we need love. He is not projecting a return or new prominence of the occult, but rather the inspiration of divinity that is derived from intuition.

Lorie predicts a new world that has our individual magic. The development of a new Eden!

In his book "Revelation" Peter Lorie states: "Profound religiousness entails a willingness to sample inner divinity, to listen to our God inside ourselves, and know that we are each of the central source of love and enlightenment-- that life gives birth to itself simply out of an intense passion for more life and that each individual is simply an opportunity for greater human awakening. "

In the future, intuition will play a stronger role. The great human awakening might include the presence of God living within us bringing joy and bliss.

OUR DIVINITY

We are all divine beings. We are all one. Realizing and recognizing the divinity in every single person creates understanding and compassion. The divinity we share in all our hearts is our human oneness.

A great spiritual leader, Sai Maa, teaches us that human beings all possess divine light. "Do not fight! Shine your light!" Fighting usually inspires more fighting. Light shows the way.

Love, Light, and Truth are the three major characteristics we experience and enjoy in the new paradigm. It is rapidly emerging in our new era. While we can expect resistance to oneness and difficulties in acceptance by everyone, more oneness will create better human beings and much more enjoyable lives! Resist the contamination of separateness. We are all one! It is within our community that we experience individuality and reliance on each other.

Together we can create a New Heaven and a New Earth. In our new world, many prophecies indicate earthly calamities-- dehydration, volcanic eruptions, famine, social unrest, destabilizing conflicts, war, and violence--all during the coming months or years. With such dreaded predictions, it is necessary to hold on to our hopes, dreams, and expectations of a New Heaven and a New Earth, a blessed future with an abundant reality of Love, Truth, and Light.

ONENESS

Choose to be strong and courageous rather than fearful. We are all one. We are all equal. We share the same divinity. This is the essence of enlightenment.

It is likely that everyone in the world will not suddenly and completely obtain enlightenment and become filled with love, light, truth, compassion, gratitude, balance, generosity, respectfulness, etc. However, it is possible that many human beings will come to see humanity as essentially equal and come to adopt a worldview of oneness rather than dualism.

Oneness is seeing the world in different shades of wholeness. We have exhausted the old paradigm of duality. We have much more in common than we realized. We have learned that we need each other. We have learned we are interdependent. Gradually we can change from dualism and embrace oneness.

What would happen if we just enjoyed helping or doing for others as best we can! Embracing oneness begins by seeing actions (and beliefs) as places on a continuum, rather than opposites and/or permanent separations between us. Oneness exchanges constant negative judging with enlightened understanding and compassion. We need to be discerning about what we do. Mental, non-emotional assessments, rather than constant judgements of how the other person should act is a better way to perceive differences.

What is the most important dynamic of the New Paradigm? We are moving from the old paradigm to a new paradigm in which we are learning to live in Oneness. We intend to make progress but due to our human limitations, we may also be handling duality. Eventually, we will exhaust and end the old paradigm of consistent, harmful duality. We may be in the curious position of knowing how to straddle and live in the old paradigm while we are in the process of changing from dualism to embracing oneness, loving our enemies as well as our families and friends. Embracing oneness is learning to see actions and the beliefs of others as places on a continuum rather than separations. We will experience more peace.

Speak the truth. State observations of the situation; resist judgments.

"Treat others as you wish to be treated" requires a sense of oneness. To treat others as we would like to be treated must be provided within the framework of oneness, not dualism. Take care not to bargain or place restrictions on such actions.

GETTING TO KNOW ME

Pandemic separations often kept us from being together, but we did learn about some benefits. We can now get together more deliberately and with more purpose. We learned we can be nourished by staying home and getting acquainted with ourselves. We may no longer constantly seek distractions. We have become more aware that our closest friends are ourselves and came to know more about who we are.

Our lives had become too busy. We came to realize how important our inner selves are. A spiritual life is found, not on the outside, but inside ourselves. True happiness comes from the inside. Knowing and loving oneself is central. Become more familiar with your soul, your higher self, your guide, your angel, and your true self. It is your "me" who will continue beyond this life. We do not ever really die. Our divine soul will always live.

Now we can get together again, learn and share with each other, with compassion, love, and truth!

The New Paradigm features increased inward communication with one's true self. You will have more insights and relationships with others as you communicate more with self. Oneness will become more expected and welcome. Fill your life with gratitude. You likely will be surprised at the greatness of your riches, more blessed the more gratitude you have!

We are likely to gradually develop increased trust in spiritual guidance, insights, and intuition.

GRATITUDE

Take several moments every day to express your gratitude. You will become aware of how rich your life is. You will likely come to trust your spiritual guidance and insights more than ever. Realize the wisdom of your intuition will become more valued, as much or sometimes more than facts. We will be able to intuit guideposts and steps to enlightenment in a collective awakening. A result will be an increase in providing help to one another. It is in serving others that we become truly richer.

INDIVIDUALITY AND COMMUNITY

Unity inspires many people to express their individuality. It is only natural that individuality creates notice, interest and interaction within a community. The natural result of an increase of interactions is more interdependence and growth of services to one another, boosting our understanding of community----Unity. Community. Individuality. Interaction. All are ways of living. All our ways of giving.

Can major changes in human behavior occur? Is our energy selfish, mean, competitive, or only for ourselves? Or are we thoughtful, kind, supportive, loving, caring? Can people change for the better? Are they changing? Have we already changed?

TRUTH

A welcome prediction of the New Paradigm is the return of TRUTH as a central value. Unfortunately, the truth of a particular action, event, or statement was no longer required for its truth to be announced, believed in or celebrated. The unreliability of truth may have begun with the realization that there is more than one way to look at an event or actions, which is true. However, something exists, or it doesn't. It is or it isn't. To simply give no credence to the actuality of an action or event or to say, "let's believe whatever we wish to be true because this is an age of false information." We do not want to create a world where anything can be made up, and nothing is sacred.

Not long ago, an individual or news reporter who made a statement that contained a lie would be required by the public or media to apologize and correct the error. In the last two decades, opinion was often considered equal to facts or seen as superior. This will no longer be so. Intuition and opinion are different from each other. Intuition will become stronger.

The Truth is making a comeback! The rise of the New Feminine Energy brings new respect to the truth. Feminine energy recognizes the positive aspects of forgiveness and compassion.

Each age or era of humankind tends to have its own special theories or concepts which demonstrate the high values of the particular era. For example, "The Age of Reason" was a time when everything of high value could be explained in rational terms. Miracles were shown to have realistic or scientific explanations. Similarly, during the

"Technological Age" technology commanded our attention and technological inventions and explanations grew enormously.

Considerable attention has been paid to the coming of the 21st century. What will be the new patterns of behavior? Astrologists as well as philosophers and scientists see new patterns and changes approaching. The expected ending of various natural resources being available calls us to make major changes. Overpopulation, climate changes, floods, famine, and dwindling of basic resources signal the possible end of sustained viability throughout the world!

THE NEW PARADIGM, THE NEW AGE

We must hold on to our hopes. A New Heaven and a New Earth is a blessed future where each day brings us a new reality.

Love, Truth, Light-- these are three characteristics we hope to experience and enjoy in the New Paradigm. When we realize that we are all one, we appreciate each other and share more with each other.

Consider all the extreme losses caused by climate change. We must do everything we can to preserve the world we still have. We may experience suffering due to earthquakes, fires, volcanic eruptions, famines and violence, but all will not happen to us at once.

Suffering is painful. Pain can overwhelm us. Losses can seem unbearable. Lack of food and/or shelter becomes intolerable. While often in times of suffering and pain, we receive new strength, nevertheless it can seem overpowering. Difficult times teach us compassion, honoring basic human equality and courage.

We are in a new era and a time of immense change for many reasons. We need to embrace, understand and live oneness. Personal success is being redefined. Recognition has been overvalued. We need more "downtime" to bring our spirits up.

The power of superpower and super wealth continues but is no longer unshakeable. The New Paradigm will not have the center of a new belief system! How different is that! Instead, we will become exposed to our inner divinity. Experiences from our intuition will enable a new experience in self-regulation.

We will have more healing resources. We will understand more about our brains, be much more familiar with our bodies, including knowledge of our subtle, ethereal, emotional bodies, and the sacred knowledge of our chakras, longevity, life on other planets and much more.

The vision of Jesus will be present in the New Paradigm as will the presence of guides, spiritual masters, saints, and angels. Individuals will receive blissfulness and joy from experiences of God within. There will be more concern for the heart instead of the head. Each of us will be a center for light and enlightenment. There is no place for ego in the New Paradigm but wonderful places for oneness.

In oneness, we perceive various actions and beliefs as degrees on continuums rather than either good or bad. Oneness dispels constant judging and offers support, understanding and compassion. We can use discernment, rather than judgment. The distance between spiritual and physical reality will become less and less.

Our role is to allow. The New Paradigm is full of truths and actions that are different from what we have known. It is up to us to open our hearts and heads to allow changes we may not understand and to recognize what is or may be the New Paradigm, full of love, truth and light.

We can live the lives we create on a much-improved earth, balancing feminine power with masculine power.

Eventually, the New Paradigm will bring more equality for all people, care of Mother Nature, and respect for the Divine in all people.

Love deeply. Together we will create a new earth where there is more harmony between people, technical advancement and spirituality, growth and transformation intertwining with one another

What a wonderful time to be alive!

Pandemic Parables and the New Paradigm resonates with the four key principles of the Danish philosopher, N.F.S. Grundtvig. If we really live them. The principles were identified by Professor Walter Capps who believed these basic principles could unite all people regardless of their religions or background. They can be tightly summarized as: Love life, Love nature, Love people; and Love learning.

Love Life-- Affirm Life. Life is fantastic!

Love nature- Love and protect Mother Nature. We are part of nature; she is part of us.

Love people-- We humans share our Divinity. The Divine in me honors the Divine in you.

Love Learning--Constantly grow and learn, be and do!

It is all of us who must bring the new paradigm into reality. A New Heaven and a New Earth will be our future if we help bring it into reality. There will be more harmony between technical advancement and spirituality, materialism, and spirituality, hope, growth and transformation.

And *God shall wipe away all tears from their eyes, and there shall be no more death, neither sorrow, nor crying, neither shall there be any more pain; for the former things are passed away.*

The Book of Revelation,
21:4

WELCOME TO THE NEW PARADIGM!

You are going to love it here.

APPENDIX

HARALD IBSEN
A Short Biography
By Joy Ibsen

Harald Ibsen was born in Irene, South Dakota on November 2, 1898, but raised in Denmark, where his mother returned with her three young children in 1904 following her husband's death when Harald, age 6, was the oldest and helped carry luggage and his baby brother.

In Denmark, Harald was in the Royal Guard and served at the Amalienborg Palace in Copenhagen.

Harald Ibsen's formal education consisted of The Askov Folk School in Denmark, Grand View Seminary in Des Moines, IA, from which he graduated, and a summer at Garrett Biblical Institute, Evanston, IL in 1940 where he studied psychiatry and religion.

From 1934, when he graduated from the Danish Lutheran Seminary in Des Moines, Iowa, until June 1965, Harald Ibsen served several Danish American congregations, first as a seminary graduate in Oakland, California, a mission church where the famous tenor, Lauritz Melchior, visited and sang.

Harald Ibsen graduated from the seminary during the Depression. In order to reach his first post in Oakland, he "rode the rails" from western Nebraska to the San Francisco Bay. His account of that challenging journey is a story of a faith that never left him and is included in the appendixes of the books Unafraid I and Unafraid II.

In the dusty late 30s, Harald Ibsen answered his first call to Diamond Lake, Minnesota, which has neither diamonds nor lake, but where the dew sparkles as brightly as diamonds! From there he went to Kimballton, Iowa in 1942, with its rich, hilly terrain, a Danish-American community that now has its own "Little Mermaid" fountain.

In 1948 our family moved to the Ibsen ancestral homeland of Viborg, South Dakota, where my great-grandfather originally settled as an immigrant and the love of prairie still beckons. In 1961, the Ibsen family moved to his last congregations in Kronborg, Nebraska, the beautiful country church near a dusty deserted crossroads, imaginatively named for Hamlet's elaborate castle.

Married late in life (at age 37), he and my mother, Asta Juhl Ibsen, raised 3 children--my older brother, David: me, Joy, and my younger sister, Karma. My parents lost their infant son, Paul, before I was born.

My father would often read stories to us. I grew up with Hans Christian Andersen's stories; my favorite was "The Tinder Box." Dad also liked traditional fairy tales, especially "The Three Billy Goats Gruff" which we performed regularly, each "kid" going over the piano bench bridge, smallest to largest, as Dad, who made a clever troll, snarled beneath us.

Norse mythology was embraced in our home along with Christian theology. "Listen," my father would say as we sat on the front porch during a cloudburst. "It's Thor. He's bowling."

The power in his sermons -- the power to overcome fear and to enjoy life -- is inspired in part by the work of the Danish theologian, philosopher, and educator N.F.S. Grundtvig. Grundtvig (1783-1813) was central to my father's view of life, and he continues to be a major influence in my life. (See Introduction and appendix for more information on Grundtvig.)

I wondered how my father managed to accomplish his work BC (Before Computers). He served in rural areas without a library. Fortunately, he had a good library of his own and he read and thought deeply throughout his life.

Harald Ibsen in his study in Viborg, SD. Note the picture of N.F.S. Grundtvig on the wall.

When weather permitted Harald liked to sit out of doors. We would see him looking out into space, oblivious to everything around him. Getting his attention was difficult. Religion must make sense. One needs to spend time thinking, not just reading and writing.

Sometimes my father would make illogical statements with certainty. Toward the end of my first pregnancy, Dad said the baby would be born May 24th, prior to my due date, apparently because it was his brother's birthday. Uncle Ernst lived in Denmark and had no possible connection to my baby's birth.

When we called my parents and announced Mitch's birth (on Ernst's birthday) Dad did not mention his prediction. He never made "I told you so "comments.

One comment I hear about my father: "What I remember about your Dad is his laugh. When something struck him funny, how he could laugh!"

He may be laughing now.

WHO IS N.F. S. GRUNDTVIG ?
By Joy Ibsen

Nicolai Fredrik Severin Grundtvig (1783-1812) was a Danish educator, poet, politician, theologian, bishop, philosopher, hymn writer and translator of Norse works including "Beowulf." He is very well known in Denmark and his massive work is becoming more well-known throughout the world.

Given Grundtvig's extensive writings, various talents, and enormous contributions, how can his massive work be described in a way that is succinct but also informs us of its importance and relevance? The best way I know is to concentrate on just four Grundtvigian principles, which in addition to his two core values: "Human comes First and Christian next" [or other religion] and "Freedom for Loki as well as for Thor" is a good start!

In the early nineties, I was inspired by a series of lectures at Danebod Folk Meetings in Tyler MN, given by Walter Capps (1934-1997), a professor and theologian from the University of California who became a U.S. Congressman. His overall topic was "The Future of Grundtvigianism," a surprise to me at that time. Capps stated what he saw as Grundtvig's four basic principles; all of which are accessible to human beings, regardless of religion or background.

At that time when most people were expecting a new century of ever-increasing improvements, Capps predicted numerous catastrophes occurring in the 21st century-- more violence and injustice, environmental disasters, increased ethnic prejudice, racism, and injustice, a decline in education, greater income disparity, more poverty, and suffering.

According to Capps, governments throughout the world, whether capitalist, socialist, or communist were all failing. Capps, a non-Dane, believed Grundtvig offered the best route to a healthy, more peaceful world. Ever since that lecture, I have used these principles in my life, and include them in my writings, books, and presentations.

Grundtvigian Principles

1. Affirmation of Life. Love Life. Life is an adventure! Life is fantastic! Love yourself! Love everyone! You and I are meant to be here! Recognize and celebrate creation. Honor life's goodness. Accept and love the world as it is, realizing with our help the world can be transformed! Do not get lost in a constant fabrication of what should/could be. Enjoy the world as it is.

    We humans are not mechanistic puppets. We have free will! FREE WILL! We can make what we believe needs to happen-- actually happen! We are accountable! Let's go for it.

    Enjoying life is not about perfection, but rather it is about living in gratitude, having hope, taking pleasure in what you have, and cherishing who you are rather than self-judging yourself and/or judging others.

    Live in gratitude. Be thankful you are alive-- from the top of your head down to the bottom of your live toes! Place gratitude in every organ and individual cell of your body!

2. Stay as Close as Possible to Nature. This is not simply a matter of being attentive to our environment. It is realizing we are *part* of nature! We are made of the same "stuff."

Humans are distinguished from animals and plant life in their ability to speak. We celebrate "The Word." We respect and love the world because "God (or whatever word you use-- Source, Yahweh, etc.) so loved the world." We care for it, not just because we need it to survive but because of who/what we are-- human beings being human. There is no power on earth greater than love. The more we love and respect nature, the more tremendously we will grow and thrive.

3. Third is the principle of "The Goodness and Beauty of Ordinary Life." Every life is both ordinary and extraordinary. Notice the goodness of ordinary people every day of your life! Each of us is "one in a million" and each of us is "one in a million." The trick is to learn to be both at the same time. This is unified--oneness, humility, and self-fulfillment. Oneness comes from how we live our lives. Living is not something artificial based on an institution. There is great integrity and creativity in working with one's hands, engaging in the arts, crafts, and building projects. Happiness? Rather than being idealistic, we find meaning and happiness in our relationships with ourselves, and one another, and in doing what we are called to do.

4. Fourth is the principle of "Lifelong Learning and Education." All of us need to be constantly learning, not only acquiring facts and degrees in order to make a living, important as that is. Universal education for *life* is necessary in order for democracy to thrive. We need to learn about our world, ourselves, our history. We need to learn who we are and be who we are. A super quick overview of Grundtvig's primary contributions to living a

better way of life can be gleaned by considering two core beliefs: from his early work as noted by Ove Korsgaard in (Korsgaard, Ove. 2014. *N.F.S. Grundtvig-- as a Political Thinker*, translated by Edward Broadbridge. Copenhagen: Diof Publishing)

A. Human First simply means recognizing the fact that we are all human beings. It is a historical fact that human beings came before any religion. We can learn to relate to each other-- human beings to human being-- first and foremost, without regard to race, religion, social status, ethnicity or any other characteristics.

Each and every human being has the capacity to contribute to society. Whoever and wherever we live or come from, whatever we believe, we can contribute to society and live peacefully together based on the simple fact that we are all human! We do not share the same religion, but as human beings, we come from a common source. We can live together peacefully if we first acknowledge each other as fellow human beings. We are each part of what Grundtvig called "the Divine Experiment." This is not to say that beings other than humans are not divine. Religion and other spiritual avenues can help us work together for the common good of all people. Spirituality can be meaningful within and outside of organized religion.

B. Grundtvig honored ancient religions. He is famous for the statement, "Freedom for Loki as well as for Thor", the major Viking god of thunder and the sky who wields a magic hammer. Thor is also the god of truth.

His influence is going to be greatly felt in the New Paradigm.

Loki is a Norse god, an unethical trickster, the god of lies and deceit who causes great mischief. Grundtvig's definition of freedom insists on equal accountability for those who are cunning and untrustworthy as well as those who hold powerful, reputable, honorable positions. Without equal justice, there is no justice.

Another element of Grundtvig's definition of freedom has to do with a basic limitation. "My freedom is not freedom if it has a negative effect on your freedom." (And vice versa) "If your freedom negates my freedom, it is not freedom!" What we do to others we do to ourselves. There is more to Grundtvig than these two core beliefs and I hope you will pursue learning more about his teachings.

FOLK SCHOOLS

N.F.S. Grundtvig (1783-1872) is known as the founder of the folk schools. Grundtvig is known for his belief that a good education embraces the idea of a living community and fellowship, ideas which have informed educational movements all over the world-- it is education not just for making a living, but for enjoying life. He is also known as the father of Public education. He was an early voice against slavery and far ahead of his time for women's rights. He was very complex-- an educator, poet, politician, seer, bishop, theologian, philosopher, and hymn writer (more than 1500 hymns, many of which are still sung today).

Folk schools have had a major effect in the United States. especially in the civil rights movement and the Highlander Folk School   At a Whitehouse dinner in 2013, President Barack Obama spoke about N.F.S. Grundtvig and the effect of the folk schools on Civil Rights. "I might not be here if it were not for the efforts of those who attended Highlander." Myles Horton was a man from Tennessee who co-founded the Highlander Folk School.   Rosa Parks attended the folk school the summer before she refused to give up her seat on a bus. Pete Seeger who also attended Highlander Folk School and Zilphia Horton (Myles's wife) adapted an old Baptist Hymn to sing at the folk school, "We Shall Overcome," which became the theme song of the civil rights movement. John Lewis and Dr. Martin Luther King and Eleanor Roosevelt were also influenced and visited and supported Highlander Folk School which was closed and moved because the school practiced integration which was then against the law. It is now a research center. Myles Horton had major responsibilities for organizing the citizenship schools which is said to have enabled 100,000 people to be educated enough to vote!

N.F.S Grundtvig is not well known in the United States, but his influence should not be underestimated. The lectures at Danebod, and in folk schools around the world, are usually not limited to a particular national or cultural topic, but rather on a variety of diverse subjects such as climate change, music, the justice system, history, artificial intelligence, and Native American spirituality.

At Danebod Folk School we enjoy folk dancing, lectures, musical presentations, and story time in the afternoon. This is our world; God is in our world. The world is precious, and we need to learn more about it and help create the future. Professor Walter Capps (University of

California, Santa Barbara) proposed that in Grundtvig we find ways to meet virtually all of the great challenges we face today. He rightly predicted that the problems of ecology, diversity, ethnicity, poverty, and violence would become much worse in the 21st century. In affirming our love of nature and in the "Human First" (human being to human being) philosophy, we meet and celebrate one another. Together, we find ways to meet the challenges before us.

It is necessary, however, to honor all four principles. It is inadequate to adopt or focus exclusively on one or two of these principles. We must practice all four.

An eternal optimist, in spite of the difficult times we have experienced since this new millennium began, I feel we may well be rounding the bend and making progress toward a more humane and spiritual world, one which resonates with the four Grundtvigian principles.

April 2024
Joy Marie Ibsen

PRESIDENT OBAMA'S SPEECH ABOUT GRUNDTVIG
May 13, 2016

"Many of our Nordic friends are familiar with the great Danish pastor and philosopher Grundtvig who, among other causes, championed the idea of the Folk School-- education that was not just made available to the elite, but to the many.   Training that prepares a person for active citizenship improves society.

"Over time the Folk School Movement spread, including here to the United States. One of those schools was in the state of Tennessee. It was called the Highlander Folk School. At Highlander, especially during the 1950s, new generations of Americans came together to share their ideas and strategies for advancing civil rights, for advancing equality and justice. We know the names of some of those who were trained or participated in the Highlander school-- Ralph Abernathy, John Lewis, Dr. Martin Luther King, Jr.

"They were all shaped in part by Highlander and the teachings of the great Nordic Philosopher, and they ended up having a ripple effect on the Civil Rights movement and ultimately on making America a better place. We would not have been here had it not been for that stone that was thrown in the lake and created ripples of hope that ultimately spread across the ocean to the United States of America. I might not be standing here were it not for the efforts of people like Ella Baker and the others who participated in the Highlander Folk School.

"So, that's just one small measure of the enormous, positive influence that our Nordic friends have had on our country. It's part of the reason why we so value your friendship, and I've said it before and I will repeat, they punch above their weight. In their values, in their contributions, not just to make their own countries function well, but to make the whole world a better place make them one of our most valuable partners everywhere in the world. We are very grateful for the outstanding work that they do. So I propose a toast. To the friendship between us and the values that we share, and that nations keep standing together and mending in part for the moral universe and stretching for just and peace and equality for all. Skal! Cheers."

ACKNOWLEDGEMENTS

This new Unafraid III "Pandemic Parables" was written after COVID-19 turned our world topsy-turvy. Very little seems to be written about how this has affected us and what the future might be like. I wanted to write about people during the pandemic--and use parables (wisdom stories) as a framework to communicate the spiritual as well as cultural changes that affected all of us. The unexpected reactions to the Pandemic caused an entire ending to the story of the pandemic's effects, the beginnings and subsequent changes brought on by the New Paradigm.

I became a member of the newly formed Vineyard Writer's Club shortly after moving to Albuquerque. NM in 2018. My special thanks to my fellow writers (Delora and Bob Saviteer, Margaret Tessler, Bill Cissna, Don Lenef, and newer members Janet Wandel, Jannie De-Angelis, Ray Harrington, and Bill Shore) for their ideas, feedback, and encouragement as we lived and wrote together, gradually finding our way through early and late "pandemic confusion." What a pleasure to listen to one another's writing projects as we traveled our life journeys.

I greatly appreciate the critiques and support from my good friend, The Rev. David Hyndman, my sister Karma Ibsen, my daughter Thea Martin, and sons Mitch Martin and Noah Martin. A grateful thanks to my husband, Don Lenef, for his consistent support throughout the years. Unfortunately, he did not live to see the published work of Pandemic Parables and the New Paradigm.. Thank you, my dear friend, Kay Linquist, for assisting with reviewing the final manuscript, and to Mary Morgan for her technical support and for designing the cover.

I am blessed and grateful for Sai Maa and especially for her teachings about the New Paradigm and balancing feminine and masculine energy on earth. It absolutely wouldn't have been possible to write and publish my books without the spiritual support I have received. In addition to Sao Maa, my deepest gratitude to spiritual teachers, Megan McGeowin and all my fellow Mary Magdalenas.

For more about Sai Maa, see the website Awakened Life.com and/or listen to her presentations on YouTube. I thank my committed fellow students, dear friends, and loving family for your blessings, prayers, intentions, insights, and support.

April 2025
Joy Marie Ibsen

ABOUT THE AUTHOR

Joy Ibsen now lives in Lisle, Illinois after moving closer to family members in 2024. Previously she and her husband, Don Lenef, lived in Albuquerque, New Mexico, and Michigan's Upper Peninsula where they enjoyed the shores of Lake Superior and the Porcupine Mountains. They resided in Trout Creek, Michigan and in Evanston and Oak Park, Illinois. The couple have five children and five grandchildren between them.

Joy grew up in Danish-American communities in Minnesota, Iowa, and South Dakota. She has a passion for the work of N.F.S. Grundtvig, the Danish theologian, philosopher, politician, educator, poet and hymn writer. For twelve years she was the editor of the only Grundtvigian journal in the United States, *Church and Life*. In 2013 Joy spent two months in Denmark studying Grundtvig's current relevance to modern life by interviewing thirty-two Danish Grundtvigians.

She graduated from high school in Viborg, South Dakota, attended Grand View University in Des Moines, Iowa, graduated from Shimer College, then in Mount Carroll, Illinois, and pursued graduate studies at the University of Chicago Divinity School where she had two classes with theologian Paul Tillich. She has a certificate in Lay Ministry from the School of Theology, University of the South.

Her varied career includes serving as a caseworker for public aid recipients in Chicago's Woodlawn ghetto; teaching GED to Vietnam-bound soldiers at Fifth Army Headquarters, Chicago; teaching English, literature and theater to students at St. Katherines/St Mark's preparatory school in Davenport, Iowa; as chief planner for the Model Cities Program in Rock

Island, Illinois; fundraising and management consulting for community, education and healthcare organizations. She spent 18 years heading development offices at Mount Sinai, Methodist, and Swedish Covenant hospitals in Chicago. In the Upper Peninsula, Joy taught piano lessons and served as the church organist.

In December 2022, Joy was initiated as a Mary Magdalena practitioner under the auspices of Sai Maa. She has also studied with Megan McGeowin, Jeni Miller, Nancy French, and Gwen Osborn.

Joy's other published books include *The Declaration of Interdependence, Here and Hereafter, The Eternity Connection; Songs of Denmark: Songs to Live by; Unafraid, I; Unafraid II, Poetry in the Porkies, and a children's book, Reginald, The Cat who Couldn't Sleep.*.

"I learned to ride a bike, and now a trike!"

www.ingramcontent.com/pod-product-compliance
Lightning Source LLC
Chambersburg PA
CBHW071731120626
46550CB00002B/476